THREE PLAYS

FRANK DUNNE

UISCE EDITIONS

First published in 2009

UISCE EDITIONS
15 Dinan Way, Exmouth, Devon EX8 4EZ, UK

ISBN 978-0-9563197-0-8

Printed in Great Britain by
Short Run Press Limited, Exeter, Devon.

CONTENTS

PLAYERS AND PAINTED STAGE

The first production of Players and Painted Stage took place in Bristol under the management of Show of Strength on September 28th 1995 with the following cast:

Matt Stuart Hutchison
Nan Anne Kavanagh
Bernard Paul Nicholson
Alec Louis Dempsey
Ellen Nicola Goodchild
Ted Aidan Dooley
Tim Nick Thomas
Billy Alan Moore

The play was directed by Caroline Hunt.
The setting was designed by Elizabeth Bowden.
The lighting was designed by Andy Collins.
The creative producer of Show of Strength is Sheila Hannon.

> Players and painted stage took all my love,
> And not those things that they were emblems of.
> – W. B. Yeats

PLAYERS AND PAINTED STAGE

Characters

Matthew Monahan, leading man and proprietor of the company
Nan, his wife
Bernard, English character actor
Alec, young Irish actor
Ellen, young English actress
Ted, young Irish actor and stage manager
Tim, the local caretaker of the hall
Billy, middle aged Irish actor

The play takes place on the stage of a hall in a small town on the east coast of Ireland in the early Sixties.

Act One: Tuesday morning.
Act Two: Thursday morning and evening.

ACT ONE

Scene one. *Tuesday morning. A bare stage, except for some chairs, a table, a skip, a stage lamp stand. A few scenery flats lie against the back wall. A pile of scripts on the table, a Roman standard propped against the skip. Matt enters reading a script, mouthing lines. He sits. After a moment Nan enters, stitching a prop dress. She sits. A pause. Bernard enters, reading a newspaper. He sits. Ted crosses from left to right carrying a floodlight stand. He exits right.*

Matt (*Still looking at his script*) Ready.

Ted (*Off*) Ready.

Bernard (*Still reading the newspaper*) Yes: ready. Been ready for hours.

Matt (*Still in his script*) Ready to start.

Ted (*Returning from right to left with a spotlight: shouting*) Ready to start.

Bernard (*Still in his newspaper*) Been ready to start for bloody hours.

Nan We can't start. Everyone's missing.

Matt Everyone's missing, Ted.

Ted (*Off*) Who's missing?

Nan Alec's missing.

Matt Alec's missing, Ted.

Nan Ellen's missing.

Matt Ellen's missing, Ted.

Bernard She's always bloody missing.

Nan Leonard's missing.

Matt Leonard's –

Ted (*Entering with a roll of electric cable in his hand*) I know Leonard's missing. He's been missing all morning. He hasn't been near the hall since last night.

Matt Theatre, Ted, theatre. I've never played in a hall, dear boy, in all my life.

Bernard Call this hen house a theatre. I've seen cow sheds in better shape than this.

Matt Where is he, Ted? Where is Leonard?

Nan I know where.

Matt Where?

Nan Gone.

Matt Gone?

Nan Scarpered. I recognized the signs. He's done it before on us.

Matt He wouldn't. He promised me never again. I took him back on that condition.

Nan I don't care what you took him back on. After his big dry last night I knew we were in for trouble.

Matt Did he say anything to anybody? Ted, did he say anything to you?

Ted No, Mr Monahan, he didn't say anything to me.

Matt Did he say anything to you, Bernard?

Bernard (*Still stuck in his newspaper*) Did who say anything to me?

Matt Leonard.

Bernard He's always saying things to me. Bloody rubbish half of it.

Matt Yes, but about his dry. Was he worried about his dry?

Bernard We were *all* worried about his dry. It brought the bloody play to a halt.

Matt Have you tried his digs, Ted?

Ted No, Mr Monahan.

Matt Try his digs. He may have overslept.

Nan He never oversleeps.

Matt You try, Ted. We'll get on with the rehearsal.

Ted exits

Nan We can't get on with the rehearsal. Not without Ted. Who's going to prompt?

Matt They shouldn't need a prompt. We've done Caesar before. We did it on the Spring tour.

Nan And the others aren't here.

Matt Where are they? Where are the others, Ted? (*Pause: then shouting*) Ted!

Ted (*Running in*) Yes, Mr Monahan?

Matt Where were you?

Ted You told me to go to Leonard's digs.

Matt Well, before you go, find out where the others are.

Ted Ellen's in the dressing room.

Matt Well, get her then, get her.

Ted She says she's too ill to rehearse.

Matt What's the matter with her?

Ted Her pipe again.

Matt Her what?

Ted That tube thing in her neck that's always playing her up.

Nan Her thyroid gland.

Bernard Her thyroid gland. Her elongated neck. Her housemaid's bloody knee. She's never right, that one isn't.

Matt Well, gland or no gland, she's got to rehearse.

Nan I don't see the point of rehearsing. I think it's ridiculous, absolutely nonsensical, trying to do Julius Caesar with seven actors. Just as it's absurd doing Merchant of Venice with seven actors.

Bernard Six, if wobbly old Leonard's done a bunk again.

Nan There you are. We're down to six actors now. How can we do Julius Caesar with six actors?

Matt We've always done Julius Caesar. We always will do Julius Caesar. Apart from anything else, it's what the schools and convents want to see.

Bernard I doubt if they want to see the pint-sized version we do.

Matt We retain the essentials, Bernard, dear. That's what's important.

Nan Ted, please find Alec and Ellen. Tell them they're late for rehearsal. Then go to Leonard's digs, but I know you won't find him.

Ted (*Going off and calling*) Alec, Ellen, you're late for rehearsal.

Pause. Nan takes a piece of paper from her pocket.

Nan (*To Matt*) Could you throw your eye over this, Matt, before I send it to the printers.

Matt What is it?

Nan The poster for the next few weeks. I presume you don't intend to make any changes. Sunday: Rebecca. Monday: Jane Eyre. Tuesday: Gaslight. Wednesday: Merchant. Thursday: Arms and the Man. Friday: Ideal Husband. And Saturday: Pygmalion. Is that O.K.?

Bernard It'll be thrown haywire if Leonard's gone.

Nan God, yes, it will. I'd better hang on to it till we know.

Bernard Who's to play Caesar if he's gone?

Matt He may *not* have gone.

Nan He's gone.

Bernard I quite see it's feasible doing it with nine tenths of the parts telescoped into seven, but I fail to understand how we can get over the problem of not having a Caesar.

Matt We must wait and see.

Bernard After all, the bloody thing *is* called Julius Caesar.

Enter Tim in tatty trousers, open necked shirt, none too clean, rolled up sleeves, carrying brush and bucket.

Tim That's a great play, Julius Caesar. I saw it once in Wicklow. The blood spouted out of him on all sides when they done him in. It was shooting out in all directions. We nearly had to put up umbrellas to stop us being drenched sitting there in the hall watching.

Nan Who are you?

Tim I, ma'am, am Tim.

Matt I'm extremely pleased to meet you, Tim. But may I enquire what exactly you are doing here?

Tim I'm washing.

Bernard Washing?

Tim And scrubbing, dusting, polishing, shining things up, rubbing things down.

Nan You are the cleaner, are you?

Tim In a way, ma'am.

Matt What do you mean – in a way?

Nan Are you the cleaner or aren't you?

Tim When I can fit it in, I am, ma'am.

Bernard Oh! When you can fit it in?

Tim Exactly so, sir. You see, I'm kept on the go. What with doing the spuds for Mrs Ryan and –

Nan You've come to clean the hall, have you?

Matt Yes, is that it? You've come to clean the theatre?

Tim I don't know about the theatre, sir, but you're in the right area.

Nan We've been here since Sunday morning and this is the first time we've seen you.

Tim I've been all tied up, ma'am. Every day I've been doing my level best to get down to you, but, as luck would have it, something always cropped up to get in the way. Take yesterday now –

Matt The place is absolutely filthy. How often do you clean it?

Tim Ah, well, that's a good question, sir.

Matt I mean we had to clear a mountain of dust on Sunday before I could find a spot in the dressing room where I could make up.

Tim While we're on the subject of the dressing room, sir, would you like me to give you a word of warning?

Matt Warning?

Tim Yes, sir. About your arrangements for changing. I seen on my way up ye're all together in the same room.

Matt Well, of course we're all together in the same room, dear boy, there's nowhere else for us to go.

Nan We have a curtain across the centre of the room dividing the men from the women.

Tim All the same, ma'am, it's a bit of an awkward situation, if you see what I mean.

Bernard I'm damned if *I* see what you mean.

Tim The clergy, sir. They're very hot on that sort of thing, After all, and there's no denying this fact, it *is* a parochial hall, when all's said and done. Father Jack is most particular about what goes on in here.

Bernard I wish he was most particular about getting it swept occasionally.

Tim Father Jack keeps a sharp look out for any – well, you know what I mean.

Matt No, I do *not* know what you mean.

Tim Goings on – that type of thing.

Bernard Interesting? Tell us more.

Tim Take the local dramatic society, sir. They did a powerful play last February. God, it was a great drama and fierce great acting too, sir. You'd have given anything to see it, so you would.

Matt Yes, I'm sure I would.

Tim You would, sir. I never saw acting to touch it. Especially when Mr Sweeney was falling all over the shop doing his drunk act. You could have heard them laughing in Tipperary. But there was a bit of – you know, sir – in it.

Nan A bit of what?

Tim I don't like to put it into words in your presence, ma'am. But you'll know what I mean when I say there was a little too much hugging and the type of thing you'd call kissing, ma'am.

Bernard Let us be clear on this. Did the kissing and the hugging occur in the play or behind the scenes?

Tim Begod, as far as I could see, sir, it was occurring all over the bloody place. You had to watch your step rounding a corner: you never knew what you'd come upon. That's what upset Father Jack. And Father Willie as well.

Matt Father Willie?

Tim The curate, sir. He was posted to patrol the wings and the changing rooms to make sure they kept their hands off one another.

Bernard My God, what a den of debauchery we've landed ourselves in.

Tim Oh, quare things happen here, sir. That's why Father Jack and Father Willie have to be so particular.

Nan Father Jack was very particular about getting his rent for the hall in advance. He didn't seem worried about the dressing room.

Tim Ah, well, maybe he knows it's different with ye'rselves, ma'am. Being acting people ye're up to that kind of thing all the time, so it doesn't matter very much. But it's another thing altogether when it's our own crowd that's doing it. Father Jack doesn't like them to be doing it at all.

Matt Look, dear boy, could you get a move on with the cleaning?

Tim I will, sir.

Matt You see, we have a rehearsal due to start at any moment.

Tim Oh, ye've a rehearsal? Well, I won't interfere with ye. I'll take a bit of a rest and do it when ye've finished.

Nan You can be cleaning the dressing room while we are rehearsing. It could do with a good sweep.

Tim No, ma'am, the banging and the scraping might upset ye'r concentration. I know what it's like to concentrate when ye're rehearsing.

Bernard Really?

Tim Oh, God, I do, sir. The concentration the dramatic society needed for the play in February was atrocious. They couldn't have done it if there was banging and scraping going on all the time.

Ellen rushes in followed by Alec. They walk around quickly all the time while speaking.

Ellen Leave me alone!

Alec And there you were. I saw you.

Ellen I don't know what you're on about.

Alec Yes, you do, yes, you do.

Ellen I can't – I can't talk – I can't argue while this – this is paining me – (*She points to her neck*)

Alec You forgot I came off that side in Jane Eyre, didn't you? You thought you were safe. You thought it was the other side and I couldn't get round the back of the set.

Ellen My throat. It's – no, please – I can't – I really can't –

Alec And I'd be stuck there the other side while you and he, the two of you, you and that glorified baggage man, had one another on that side –

Ellen It's all – it's all here – (*She points to her throat*) And up along here – I can't – the pain – it goes up here –

Alec But you got a surprise, a sweet surprise, didn't you?

Ellen Please! No. You see – my – my throat –

Alec Oh, a sharp surprise you got when I appeared in front of you.

Ellen This pain is too – I can't – I really can't –

She exits

Alec (*To the others*) Sitting on his lap, thinking no one was looking. I saw it all. (*Following her off, shouting*) I saw it. I saw you. (*He exits*)

Tim Begod, this looks a great rehearsal. D'you mind if I stay and watch the rest of it?

Blackout

Scene Two

Tuesday morning. A few minutes later. Matt is studying his script, Bernard is reading his newspaper, Nan stitches. A long pause before speaking.

Nan She's locked herself in the loo.

Bernard He's locked himself in the prop van.

Matt Where's Ted?

Bernard Where's Leonard?

Pause

Nan Where's that fellow?

Matt What fellow?

Nan The cleaner – caretaker – whatever he is.

Bernard He's resting while we rehearse.

Matt We can't rehearse: no one's here.

Nan That's right: no one's here – onstage or in the audience.

Matt (*Looking up*) I beg your pardon?

Nan It should be our motto, these days: no one's here. We haven't had a good house, a decent house, in months.

Matt We had a good house for Jane Eyre last week.

Nan Eighty. I don't call eighty a good house.

Matt It was a receptive house. A warm house.

Bernard It was a warm house this week too. There were still only about twenty people out there.

Matt If they respond, I don't really care about how many are there. It's response that counts.

Nan Response doesn't bring in money. It doesn't pay the salaries. It doesn't pay the hall rent. Or the printing bill. Nor the bills for transport or the wood for props and scenery.

Bernard Which reminds me, darling. That cane I use in Dracula is broken.

Matt We're not doing Dracula this tour.

Bernard You said we were. You said we'd do it after a few weeks out.

Nan Dracula brings no one in these days.

Bernard Nothing brings anyone in these days. But that's beside the point. It's my best part. My only decent part.

Nan My only decent part is Lady Bracknell. We haven't done that for two years. I'm not beefing. I'm prepared to give up good parts if only we can do things that make some money.

Bernard (*Sulking slightly*) Audiences adore Dracula.

Nan They might, Bernard dear. The trouble is they don't come to see it.

Matt They don't.

Nan They don't.

Pause

We've lost money every week this tour.

Pause

Last week we were down over two hundred pounds.

Pause

This week it looks like being worse.

Pause

Matt Makes you wonder –

Nan What?

Matt – if it was worth it.

Nan If what was worth it?

Matt Coming back.

Nan Coming back to Ireland?

Matt (*A bit lost in his thoughts*) Mmm.

Nan Of course it was worth it.

Matt (*To Bernard*) Her idea, you know: coming back.
Bernard I know.
Matt At times like this one wonders.
Nan For God's sake, Matt, it hasn't been always like this. You didn't
    say was it worth it when we did those lovely Dublin seasons.
Matt We haven't done a Dublin season now for – for –
Bernard You know, my favourite was Caesar at the Gaiety.
Nan Remember that marvellous set?
Bernard Took it to the Belfast Opera House.
Nan Cork Opera House.
Matt Yes, but –
Nan Yes, but? What – what?
Matt I was – doing well. In England. The Old Vic three seasons.
    Australia. South Africa. Twice in the West End.
Bernard You always wanted to come back, Nan, didn't you?
Nan It seemed right at the time.
Matt Oh, yes, there was a time –
Bernard There was.
Matt Full houses. Queues.
Bernard Booking days ahead.
Matt Days.
Bernard Remember?
Matt Remember all those dates?
Bernard The good dates.
Matt Dates that never failed.
Bernard I remember.
Matt Mullingar.
Bernard Mullingar!
Matt Weekends Mullingar: always packed.
Bernard Jam packed.
Nan Dundalk.
Matt God, yes: Dundalk. Couldn't get them all in.
Bernard Wexford: bloody good date.
Nan Except the year we hit the mission week.
Matt Wherever did we do well on mission week?
Nan Waterford: that week in the snow.
Matt The thing was –
Bernard (*Remembering some private joke*) And Limerick – the week
    the Bishop died.
Nan (*Laughing*) We were about to go up.
Matt (*Laughing*) Rest of the week – cancelled.
Bernard The whole bloody place drowned in black.
Matt Yes, but –
Nan Lost a hundred quid.
Matt – things were cheaper.
Bernard Oh, much!
Matt Less expensive.
Bernard Say that again.

Nan You could find digs for –
Matt Easily.
Nan – a few pounds.
Bernard I had digs for fifteen bob in Clonmel.
Nan Full board too.
Matt D'you see, there wasn't –
Nan No.
Bernard There wasn't.
Matt – wasn't the expense.
Bernard Everything's so bloody expensive these days.
Matt Everything.
Nan Salaries. Transport. Printing.
Bernard Laundry bills.
Nan Hire of halls.
Matt Yes: theatre rents.
Bernard Digs.
Matt Meals.
Nan Everything's so difficult.
Matt Every way you turn.
Nan Television.
Matt Oh, television!
Bernard That bloody thing.
Nan It kills everything.
Bernard It's killing us, that's for sure.
Matt That bloody box. Keeps them away.
Nan D'you see –
Bernard Bloody contraption.
Nan – they won't come out.
Matt Insulates them against anything good.
Bernard Anything decent.
Nan If it's raining they won't risk going out.
Matt Won't make the effort.
Bernard It's either too cold.
Nan Too hot.
Matt Too wet. Any excuse.
Nan Anything to stay in. To stay at home.
Bernard The wrong sort of plays.
Matt The right sort of plays – but not for *their* town.
Nan The wrong sort of town for our stuff.
Bernard Anything.
Nan To stay in and watch that contrivance.
Matt That box.
Bernard That bloody contraption.
Nan And – have you noticed? – there's always something on.
Matt Football.
Bernard The Eurovision bloody eisteddfod.
Nan Political appearances.
Matt Always something.

Bernard They'll find an excuse.

Nan To stay in.

Bernard Sitting, watching.

Matt Moronic.

Bernard Soporific.

Matt It kills –

Bernard Does.

Matt Everything.

Bernard Everything.

Nan Kills the lot.

Bernard The bloody lot.

Pause

Matt I'd like to know what time this rehearsal's going to start.

Pause

Nan And Billy Brien.

Matt Don't mention that fellow.

Nan Practically made it his own these days.

Bernard Still owes me four quid.

Nan Never off the thing.

Bernard Four bleedin' quid.

Pause

Nan What's the name of that thing he's in?

Matt Tripe unlimited.

Bernard Bottom of the bloody barrel.

Nan Something Road or Street, isn't it?

Bernard Rubbish bloody Road.

Nan Something Street. Or Avenue.

Matt Took him on as an electrician. Did you know that, Bernard?

Bernard I was there when he walked through the door. Begging for a job.

Matt Mallow.

Nan New Ross.

Matt Electrician! Didn't know a fuse box from a plug socket.

Nan Ah, no, he was a good electrician.

Bernard He was good at nearly blowing up every bloody place we played.

Matt Electrician and stage manager.

Bernard And that accent.

Matt No speaka de English!

Bernard Couldn't pronounce two words together properly.

Nan No, but he was a good worker and turned out to be a good electrician and stage manager.

Bernard What was it, for God's sake, the accent?

Matt West Cork.

Nan Always worked hard.

Bernard Worked hard bumping cash off me.

Nan And he worked hard too when we began to give him parts,

Bernard Couldn't act for bloody peanuts.

Nan I won't have that, no, I won't have that. Be fair, Bernard.

Matt His first part – wasn't it? – was in Hamlet.

Nan Macbeth.

Matt Bernardo in Hamlet.

Nan The Porter in Macbeth. You said it wouldn't matter in a Cork accent.

Bernard Thank God I remember nothing of that. The Porter in a Cork accent!

Nan But he didn't play it in a Cork accent, Bernard. He was able to lose it. Straight away we saw he was a good actor.

Bernard Good?

Nan Very good, as a matter of fact. We soon discovered that.

Matt In certain things, certain parts –

Bernard Oh, in *certain* parts –

Nan He was very good. No use trying to deny that fact. A very good actor.

> *Pause*

Bernard They had him on last night in the digs while I was trying to have my tea.

Nan Oh, they all watch him – in every county in the land.

Bernard Couldn't enjoy my boiled egg. Gave me indigestion.

> *Pause*

Nan You know –

Matt Yes?

Nan What if – ?

Bernard Yes?

Nan Well. (*Pause*) Listen. Do you think – ? Oh, I don't know.

Matt What?

Bernard What you on about, Nan?

Nan Suppose we asked – the thought just occurred to me – suppose –

Matt Suppose what?

Nan Suppose we invited Billy to make a guest appearance.

Matt (*Looking up*) What?

Bernard (*Looking up*) What?

Nan A guest appearance with the company. He'd be a draw. Bill him as the star of that Road thing or that Street thing – whatever it's called. Everyone watches it. Is there a digs we've been in these last three months where they haven't been gawping at him on the television? Billy could pack them in if he agreed to do something with us.

Matt What – if it's not an awkward question – would he play?

Nan We could talk about that. Something good, something big.

Bernard Such as?

Nan Oh, I don't know, Bernard. Maybe – Rochester.

Matt (*Almost exploding*) Rochester?

Nan It's just a suggestion.

Matt Rochester is *my* part!

Nan Then something we don't normally do. Something with a good meaty part for Billy.

Matt And what about me? What about a good meaty part for me? After all, it *is* my company. We happen to be known as the Monahan Players.

Nan Well, of course, you must have something good too, Matt.

Bernard And what about *me*? Am I to play second fiddle to that incompetent bloody sparks, who tried to blow us all up when he plugged the wrong wires in the wrong holes in Enniscorthy?

Nan It was Letterkenny, Bernard.

Bernard I don't care where it was. I am not acting as a bit player to a fellow who couldn't even figure out his arse from his earth wire.

Nan The whole point of the exercise is to have Billy as a draw. Business would probably be very good. I hate to sound mundane, my dears, but we might make some money.

Matt I have been in this business for over forty years. I do not need a transposed electrician to bring in the audience. I can do that on my own. My name means something throughout this country.

Nan I suppose that's why we are playing to empty houses every night.

Matt I have never played to an empty house.

Nan Small houses then. Sparse houses. Meagre and thin.

Matt I do not measure an audience by its size. Never have. But that does not mean I can't pull them in when I have to.

Nan You have to now, Matt. Else we'll close up shop. Every week we're making up losses from our savings. And we need our savings, Matt. The years aren't falling off us.

Matt What does that mean?

Nan It means we're not getting any younger.

Matt Younger? Older? I refuse to recognize those words. I go on to the day I drop. I've more energy now, more zest, than I had twenty years ago. My work is better, richer. I feel it. Everyone – everyone who knows about acting – tells me so. I could act people half my age into a cocked hat. By God, the audience wouldn't want to look at them when I appear on the stage. Older? Younger? Such words are for civil servants, accountants, nine to five cannon-fodder. They mean nothing in the theatre. Who ever heard of a pro, a real pro, retiring? Don't bore me with that nonsense. Look at Bernard there. Is he old? Is he thinking of growing roses?

Bernard Roses? Why roses?

Matt You're not thinking of retiring, are you, Bernard?

Bernard Retiring?

Matt Of course you're not.

Bernard Oh, I don't know. Not that I'd want to cultivate roses, mind.

Matt *We* do not retire.

Bernard I never could stand bloody roses.

Nan We can't go on forever. None of us can.

Bernard I've got a thing about them: roses. They always make me think of jam gone off. Jam with flies in it.

Alec rushes in, shouting.

Alec A week's notice!

Matt I beg your – ?

Alec As agreed in my contract. A week's notice on either side. I'm giving in mine. I will leave, terminate my contract, a week Saturday.

Matt You're leaving?

Nan But why, Alec?

Matt Yes, why, dear boy?

Alec She. That woman. That bloody woman. You know. You wouldn't – you wouldn't believe the things. Talk about – well. If ever, and I mean if ever, if ever there was a bitch. And when I say a bitch –

Bernard You mean a bitch.

Alec I do mean a bitch, Bernard. I mean that. Just that. A real, fully paid-up, first-class bitch.

Matt But who are you talking about, my dear boy?

Bernard Who d'you think, old man? Nell bloody Gwynn?

Alec Her. That – that – well, do I have to tell you? Do I have to spell it out?

Nan You mean Ellen?

Alec Ellen! I can't even say her name. And when I say I can't even say her name, I mean – well, you know what I mean. It sticks. (*He points to his throat*) It sticks here.

Matt I don't understand. What sticks?

Bernard Her name, old man.

Matt Ellen? I think it's quite a nice name.

Alec (*This makes Alec even angrier*) Nice? Nice?

Matt Yes, quite nice.

Alec It's a crappy name. Crappy. And when I say crappy —

Bernard Yes, yes, we know.

Alec Talk about devious. I mean devious doesn't even describe what I mean. And the joke is – the joke is –

Matt The joke is?

Bernard Yes, do tell us what the joke is.

Alec The joke is we're supposed to be engaged.

Bernard That's the joke?

Alec Did you know we were engaged, Nan?

Nan Yes, I think someone told me.

Bernard No one told me.

Matt I had no idea.

Alec Oh, yes, we're engaged. She wears my engagement ring. Haven't you seen it?

Bernard No, I haven't.

Matt I certainly haven't.

Alec We're supposed to be getting married next year. I've met her family in Manchester. She's met my mother in Dublin. It's all arranged.

Bernard When's the wedding taking place?

Alec It's *not* taking place, Bernard. Never. Ever. It's off – off. And when I say off –

Matt It's off, is it? I didn't even know it was on.

Alec It's not on, Matt, it's not on. I wouldn't marry her now if you paid me a thousand quid.

Matt I'm afraid I haven't got a thousand quid, dear boy.

Alec What do you think I caught her at last night? Necking with that bloke over there. (*He points to UL*) She thought I came off there (*He points to UR*) in that scene. So did he.

Bernard So did I. You *were* supposed to go off there in that scene. (*Bernard points to UR*) You threw the bloody lot of us when you vanished out there. (*He points to UL*)

Matt He didn't throw me. It would take more than that to throw me.

Nan He couldn't have thrown you. You weren't on in that scene.

Alec That's where I was clever, Bernard. I knew they knew – I knew they knew, or they thought they knew, that I didn't know they were there in that corner on that side. (*He points to UL*)

Matt They knew that, did they?

Alec No, Matt. They only thought they knew.

Matt Oh, I see.

Bernard Damned if I do.

Alec But. And it's a big but. I *knew* they were there. Something told me. I felt it. So. Off I went. I won't tell you what I saw.

Bernard Pity.

Alec (*Suddenly blurting it out loudly*) There she was almost on top of him. And when I say almost – well, you can use your imagination.

Nan I didn't know Ted was interested in Ellen.

Alec He's nuts about her. Never stops chasing her. But I'm warning him, warning him here and now –

Bernard There's no point in warning him. He's not here.

Alec He isn't?

Bernard No.

Alec Where is he?

Nan Gone to look for Leonard.

Alec Where's Leonard?

Nan We think left.

Alec Left?

Bernard Scarpered.

Alec No! Jesus.

Nan He's done it before on us. Long before you joined the company, Alec.

Alec Scarpered? Christ.

Nan Yes: we think so.

Alec What's going to happen?

Nan About what?

Alec About his parts.

Nan Double them. Talk round them. Like we always do. Where we can't we cancel the plays concerned.

Bernard So you see, old man, it isn't a good time to leave.

Alec Well, yes, I see that, yes. I understand that, yes, Bernard. But her and him. She and he. I mean, Well. And when I say –

Nan We do rather need you at the moment, Alec.

Alec Yes. Well. O.K. Until you get a replacement for Leonard. If he *has* gone. All right.

Nan Thanks.

Alec But don't ask me to have anything to do with her. Don't ask me. Not with that –

Nan We won't. (*To Matt and Bernard*) Will we tell Alec what we were talking about when he came in?

Matt I can't remember what we were talking about.

Bernard We were talking about roses.

Alec Roses?

Bernard Matt was encouraging me to grow roses.

Matt Impossible. I don't know the first thing about roses.

Nan No – we were talking about Billy.

Alec Billy who?

Nan Billy Brien.

Matt Our one time electrician.

Alec Oh, big star Billy!

Nan Do you know what we were discussing? Tell us what you think, Alec. We were playing with the idea of inviting him to return.

Matt I wasn't playing with the idea. I don't want him to return.

Alec Return? For what?

Nan To play with us of course. Oh, just in one production. Or perhaps two.

Matt Two? Why not make it three or four? Or let him take over the company!

Alec You've lost me, I'm afraid.

Nan Look, Alec, we're losing money hand over fist every week. We need something to improve the business, else we'll just have to pack up. Now the idea occurred to us –

Matt No, it didn't. It occurred to you.

Nan All right, it occurred to me. Perhaps if we invited Billy back he might pack them in. He's very popular on the television.

Alec Yeah, in the pub last night they were going on about him. Our only claim to fame as a company, as far as the locals are concerned, is that we discovered Billy Brien.

Nan There you are: they'd be bound to come and see him. And, you know how it is, the word spreads from town to town. They'll hear how Billy was with us and how everyone wanted to see him. That'll be good for business. It will be a good advertisement for the company.

Alec Aye, and Billy might be able to give us a few tips about the telly. I wouldn't mind getting in there and picking up a few well paid jobs. (*He rubs his hands together, then turns to Matt and Bernard*) Fab! Aye, it might do us all a bit of good. And when I say –

Matt I have no wish to be done a bit of good in that respect, thank you very much. I once did a television in London. I do not intend to repeat the experience. Nothing but cables and tubes and wires over you head, under your feet, microphones rammed down your gullet, entrapped by machinery. No, thank you!

Bernard They asked me to do a television.

Alec I didn't know you'd been on television, Bernard.

Bernard I haven't. I told them to lose themselves. They wanted me to go to Manchester to play a decaying vicar, who'd lost all power of speech and movement.

Alec A non speaking part?

Bernard A non moving part would be more bloody like it.

Alec But the money's good, Bernard. And you do it all in a few days. No offence, Matt, no offence, Nan, but you'd earn in a week in telly more than you'd earn in a year on tour.

Nan If the business was better we could pay more, dear.

Alec D'you think Billy would bring them in?

Nan It's worth a try.

Alec Will he come?

Nan Last time he was down he said he'd give anything to work with us again. I think he meant it. Today I suddenly remembered what he'd said.

Alec And every interview he gives he never fails to mention the Monahan Players and the great time he had with you. The happiest days of his life, he called them.

Matt The happiest days of his life buggering up my lighting plots.

Nan Unfair. He turned out to be a good electrician.

Matt If you say so.

Nan And he developed into a good actor.

Alec He *is* a good actor. You have to give him that.

Matt And talking of giving him things. What sort of money are we expected to pay him for the great privilege of having him appear with us?

Bernard He'll demand a big fee and pocket any profit.

Matt If there *is* a profit – which I doubt.

Nan Oh, it's most unlikely he will insist on a big fee. After all, he makes a lot of money nowadays.

Alec Aye, he's in the money, sure enough.

Bernard That's when those buggers make sure of a fat fee.

Nan Well, when I write to him I'll make it plain that the reason he is coming is to help the company. I'm sure he will look on it as more of a prestige thing than an opportunity to make money.

Alec He might even do it for nothing.

Nan Yes, you know him, Alec. You and he got on very well last time he came down to see us. You'll enjoy having him back.

Alec It'll be the best thing that's happened to us. Lift us out of our rut.

Matt *I* am not in a rut.

Nan Oh, Alec means it'll be good for the company.

Alec Great. (*He goes to go off, then stops, his back to the audience*) Hold it. Not so great. (*He turns to them*) Not – so – great.

Nan Not?

Alec Not.

Bernard Oh.

Alec No. That time he came down to see us. Who was he pawing and patting all the time?

Matt Who?

Bernard Not me, thank Christ.

Alec Who? She. Her. That's who.

Bernard Ellen?

Alec Her.

Nan Was he?

Alec Shooting her the big line. The big star line.

Nan I didn't notice.

Alec That crap. And did she love it!

Bernard Did she?

Alec Did she what! She lapped up every minute of it. So if he comes anywhere near the place, I'm off. Count me out. If he's coming you can accept my notice right now. And when I say –

Bernard Yes.

Alec You know.

Bernard We do.

Alec Right. (*Pause*) Right.

(*Alec exits quickly. Pause*)

Matt What was all that about?

Nan (*Going out*) Alec's opposed to inviting Billy.

Matt *I'm* opposed to inviting Billy.

Bernard He thinks he fancies Ellen.

Matt I thought it was Ted he thinks fancies Ellen.

Bernard And he thinks she fancies him.

Matt Who?

Bernard Billy.

Matt I thought it was Ted she fancies.

Bernard She does.

Matt Oh. (*Pause*) Well, thank you, Bernard. That's all very – yes, very – (*Pause*) (*Going out*) I'm glad you've cleared all that up.

Tim enters. Bernard picks up a chocolate wrapper and hands it to Tim as he goes out.

Bernard (*Going out*) There you are, old boy. I've made a start for you.

Tim (*Looking after Bernard*) That was very kind of you, sir.

He chucks the wrapper on to the floor. Enter Ellen from the other side.

Ellen Oh, isn't the rehearsal on?

Tim Nothing's on, ma'am. Just me.

Ellen Who are you?

Tim Tim, ma'am.

Ellen Are you looking for someone?

Tim I don't think I am, ma'am.

Ellen Stop calling me, ma'am. I am not married.

Tim Well, I wouldn't give up hope yet, miss. Sure, you're still young.

Ellen Please. (*Pointing to her neck*) I have the – the most awful pain. I – I do not wish to discuss marriage with you.

Tim Ah, I'm married already, miss.

Ellen No, please, listen –

Tim So I'm off the menu as far as that's concerned.

Ellen Of course I didn't mean – it's just – you know – discussing marriage with a stranger –

Tim Sure, I'm no stranger. Certainly no stranger to this oul' hall. Near on thirty years here now.

Ellen Oh, you're the caretaker?

Tim If you wish to put it like that, miss.

Ellen But we haven't seen you all week. You never clean up after the audience.

Tim The audience in this town have no regard for tidiness. They don't know the meaning of the word.

Ellen You never sweep the dressing room.

Tim Oh, I have to be careful when and at what time I tackle the sweeping, miss. Th' oul' elbow is inclined to give out if I indulge in too much sweeping.

Ellen Please. I can't carry on a conversation with this pain. (*Points to her throat*) You see, it sort of –

Tim I know, I know. A divil when it starts. (*Points to his back*) I get it here.

Ellen Where?

Tim (*Coming to her*) Here.

Ellen (*Pointing to her throat*) I get it here.

Tim There?

Ellen Here.

Enter Ted

Ted Where's everyone?

Ellen No idea. There's no one about but him.

Ted Who's he?

Ellen He's Tim.

Ted Tim?

Tim Tim, sir. Always have been.

Ellen He's the caretaker of the hall.

Ted I didn't know there was a caretaker.

Ellen He's been working here thirty years.

Ted I wish he'd been working here this week. The bloody place is filthy.

Tim Now I can give you an explanation for that, sir. I was just about to settle down to it, when –

Ellen where have you been?

Ted Looking for Leonard. Went to his digs. A Mrs O'Hooloran.

Tim O'Halligan.

Ted He'd gone. Without paying the rent.

Tim Mary O'Halligan won't be dancing too happy to that tune.

Ted She's going to claim it from Matt and Nan.

Tim Mary O'Halligan would.

Ellen So what are we going to do?

Ted We're all right for tonight: Leonard's not in Gaslight.

Ellen Yes, but the Merchant's tomorrow.

Ted We'll probably scrap the Merchant and repeat something,

Ellen What?

Ted I don't know: that's for Matt and Nan to decide.

Ellen Why did Leonard scarper like that?

Ted Ah, sure, he's been going to pieces of late. That dry he had last night was scary.

Ellen Jesus: don't.

Ted (*To Tim, who has come very close to them to listen*) What are you doing standing there? This is a private conversation. Haven't you any work to do? Like sweeping our dressing room?

Tim I didn't get round to that, sir, and I'll tell you for why –

Ted (*Pointing out front*) And look at that mound of fag packets and chocolate wrappers from last night.

Tim (*Looking at the same place*) Isn't it disgusting, sir. The people in this town need to go on a training course to teach them a few things about keeping a place nice and tidy.

Ted (*To Ellen*) Does he exist or am I dreaming him?

Ellen Oh, Ted, I've got such a throat.

Ted I mean – what's going to happen.

Tim (*Moving around, making a feeble attempt to dust a chair*) Nothing'll happen, sir. You'll never persuade the crowd round here to pick up their fag packets.

Ted I have to know. If we're not doing the Merchant tomorrow night, I want to know what we *are* doing. I have a set to get ready, props, furniture.

Ellen If these halls were cleaner I'm sure I'd feel better. I don't think I'll be able to go on tonight.

Ted God, don't say that. We've enough problems with Leonard gone.

Ellen I feel terrible.

Tim (*Sitting on the skip*) Begod, I don't feel too good myself, miss.

Ted (*To Ellen*) Why don't you lie down for the afternoon?

Tim Ah, there's no need, sir, I'll be O.K.

Ted Not you, you idiot.

Ellen What about the rehearsal?

Ted Arrah, what rehearsal? Sure, isn't the morning half over.

Ellen What are we supposed to be rehearsing?

Ted Matt wants to bring back Julius Caesar.

Ellen Impossible. We had cut most of the parts anyway. But with Leonard gone it'll be out of the question. I'd prefer to bring back – say – Wuthering Heights.

Tim Is there many comic bits in that one, miss? They're divils for comic bits round these parts. Especially if Mr Sweeney is in it. Mr Sweeney's the teacher up at the school, but as for th' acting, I'll tell you, even th' Abbey Theatre couldn't touch him.

Ellen I couldn't face learning new parts at the moment, Ted.

Tim Mr Sweeney, now. He's a great hand at the learning. If he forgets the words – he just makes them up. And ten times better they are too than any you'd find written in the book.

Alec appears at the back: he stands out of sight watching.

Ted (*Going to Ellen*) You don't look well.

Ellen My throat – my voice –

Tim Don't be talking about voices, miss. You should hear Mr Sweeney's voice. A terrible boom to it when he's on form.

Ted (*Putting his arm around Ellen*) Go back to the digs. Have a lie down.

Ellen Matt will go spare if I miss the rehearsal.

Ted Leave it to me. I'll say I sent you home.

Alec (*Coming down to them*) And I suppose you'll follow her. The two of you will have a nice rest all afternoon in her room.

Ted I just suggested she lie down.

Alec You suggested what?

Tim He suggested she lie down, sir.

Alec (*To Ted*) You'd like her to lie down, wouldn't you?

Tim It seems he would, sir.

Alec (*Ignoring Tim*) I know he would. You'd like her to stretch out back at your digs?

Ted No. *Her* digs.

Alec Oh, you wouldn't object going to *her* digs, wouldn't you?

Tim I'm sure he wouldn't. Sure, it's only a short step down the road.

Ted (*Loud*) Look – I only –

Ellen Please don't shout. It makes my head ache.

Alec Your head? I thought it was your throat.

Tim I think it's her head *and* her throat, sir.

Ted Her head and her throat – they both ache.

Alec (*To Ted*) How do *you* know about her head and her throat?

Ted Everyone knows about Ellen's head and throat.

Alec What do you mean by that?

Tim I had my tonsils out in 1947.

Alec (*To Ted*) What do you mean?

Tim I mean what I say: I had my tonsils out.

Ted Everyone in the company knows about Ellen's poor throat.

Alec Oh, no, you didn't mean that. You meant something else. And when I say you meant something else –

Tim You mean he meant something else.

Alec (*Loud*) I *do* mean he meant something else.

Ellen (*To Alec*) Please: stop shouting.

Alec (*Shouting*) I am not shouting! I am speaking perfectly normally. (*Speaking quietly to Tim*) I'm speaking perfectly normally, aren't I?

Tim I never heard better speaking in my life, sir.

Alec (To Ellen) There you are. I'm speaking normally. He says so. (*Pause: he turns to Tim*) Who are you? Are you a new member of the company?

Tim I'm not, sir. Though I did a fair bit of acting in my time. There was one murder drama the Dramatic Society did a few years back with Mr Sweeney getting shot in the third act. You've heard of Mr Sweeney – of course you have. His acting is famed the length and breadth of Ireland. The crowd loved the murder. A drop of blood always draws them round here. And, d'you see, I had to come in when Mr Sweeney said –

Alec What are you doing here during a rehearsal if you're not an actor?

Tim Ye're rehearsing, are ye? (*Pointing to each of them*) All that was part of a play, was it?

Ted No, it wasn't. We're not rehearsing.

Tim Begod, it's hard to tell exactly when ye are and when ye're not rehearsing.

Alec (*To Ted*) You're stage manager. What is this fellow doing on the stage?

Ted He's the caretaker.

Alec Caretaker? There isn't a caretaker in this place.

Tim Well, now, there is and there isn't, sir. D'you see, I'm never referred to in that way.

Alec In what way are you referred to?

Tim (*Scratching his head*) Now that I come to think of it, I'm seldom referred to in any way at all, sir.

Ellen (*A sharp scream*) Ooooh!

Tim (*Jumping*) God, miss, you made me jump out of my skin there.

Ted Ellen: you should see a doctor.

Alec She's seen a doctor in every bloody town we've been to. Doctors all over Ireland are writing books on her condition.

Ellen I can't go on like this.

Ted You can't.

Tim You can't, miss.

Alec She's been going on like this since the first day I met her.

Ellen (*Feeling her throat*) Dublin. The – ooh, ah – the railway station.

Alec (*Turning to Ellen*) The what? What are you talking about?

Ellen Don't you remember? Waiting on the station. To – ooh, my God, this pain – to go to – Tralee.

Alec (*Calming down*) Yes. Yes, that's right – Tralee.

Ellen To join the company.

Alec Yes: the first day we met.

Ted Aye, all right, O.K. Now, I think we should sort out –

Tim The first day ye met, was it?

Ellen Yes. We were – we were holding the same scripts.

Alec Holding the same scripts, that's correct. You were sitting on your case.

Ted Right, O.K., so let's – let's –

Tim (*To Alec*) Sitting on her case, was she, sir?

Ellen I was. Learning my lines.

Ted Look: we don't have time for all this. We – you know –

Alec We – talked.

Tim Talked, did ye?

Ellen Then – oh, oh, oooh –

Tim Then – miss?

Ellen Same digs in Tralee.

Tim You don't say so!

Ted Yeah – so, there's lots to sort out if – if we're not doing the Merchant –

Alec Great digs.

Tim I'm sure.

Ellen Great tour.

Tim Oh, I'm sure.

Alec Aye, great days. (*To Ted*) Then you came along – next tour. Never been the same since you came. Always up to something.

Ellen That's not true. Ted's not like that. Are you, Ted?

Alec Oh, no?

Ellen Are you, Ted?

Tim Are you, Ted?

Alec Yes, he is. And let me tell you I'm sick of it.

(*He suddenly snatches hold of the Roman Standard*)

Ellen Put that down.

Ted That's the Roman Standard. We might need it for Julius Caesar.

Alec I might need it for wrapping it round your frigging neck if you don't keep away from her and get out of our lives.

Ted Careful: don't break it.

Alec I'll break it across your bloody head.

Tim (*Rubbing his hands together*) Begod, this is great stuff. If you could put this on the stage you'd pack them in like sardines out there.

Ted Put it down: that's an important prop.

Alec (*Waving the standard dangerously at Ted*) It's a bit of an oul' brush handle with a strip of rotten wood nailed to it. Like all the faulty props you make.

Ellen (*Snatching the standard from Alec*) You're not safe to be out with that thing. (*To Ted*) You take it. (*She gives the standard to Ted*)

Alec (*To Ellen*) Oh, you want *him* to break it over *my* head! I see. I get the message.

Ted (*Waving the standard*) I don't want this prop damaged.

Alec (*To Ted*) Don't you bloody wave it at me like that. You jumped-up fucking stage hand.

(*He snatches the standard from Ted*)

Ellen (*Screaming*) He'll kill him. He'll kill him. (*To Tim*) Can't you do something?

Tim Begod, they're managing all right without me, miss.

Alec You do everything you can to bug me. (*Alec follows Ted around the stage: Alec waves the standard: Ted retreats: they move in a circle*) Never a proper cue. Never a prompt when I need one. Messing up my props. Buggering up the lighting when I have a good scene.

Ted It's all in your head.

Ellen Yes: all in your head. Ted doesn't bugger up your lighting any more than he does the rest of us.

Ted That's right. I bugger up Matt's lighting and Bernard's lighting as much as I do yours.

Alec (*Waving the standard: following Ted around*) It's me. Me he's after. Me he wants to humiliate.

Ellen snatches the standard from Alec: she throws it to Tim.

Ellen Here. You look after it.

Tim — surprised — catches the standard, stands holding it, not knowing what to do with it. Ted rushes at Alec, catches him as if he is going to strangle him.

Ted You're a nut case. That's what you are. A fucking nut case.

Ellen screams. Matt strides briskly in. Alec makes loud noises as if being strangled: Aah! Aah! aah!

Matt (*Coming face to face with Tim holding the Roman standard*) Ah: we've got a replacement for Leonard, have we? Excellent!

Blackout

Scene Three

Tuesday morning. Later. Alec sits on a chair. He is turned away from everyone. Matt is sitting downstage looking through a script of Julius Caesar. The Roman standard is propped against the skip. After a while Ellen enters, a handkerchief to her mouth. She sits, turns very deliberately away from Alec. Pause. Nan enters, a letter in her hand.

Nan What's happening? (*Calls off*) What's happening, Ted?

Ted (*Off*) Leonard's gone.

Nan I knew he had.

Ted (*Entering holding a screwdriver*) With the rent unpaid.

Nan I knew that too.

Ted The landlady is going to see you about it.

Nan And I knew that as well!

Matt Is there any chance of a rehearsal this morning?

Nan We can't rehearse. Leonard's gone.

Matt Leonard or no Leonard, we are going to do Caesar.

Ted Where's Bernard? Has he gone too?

Nan He had a phone call. They sent down for him from the Post Office.

Ted Nan: what are we doing tomorrow night?

Matt The Merchant.

Nan We can't. Not without Leonard.

Matt If we could start rehearsals we might have Caesar ready.

Ted It's just that I want to know. I have to sort out props and the set.

Nan One time we would have had three or four productions in reserve. Nowadays we've barely enough to fill out the week.

Matt (*Indicating Alec and Ellen*) What's the matter with those two? Are they meditating?

Nan (*To Ellen and Alec*) Have you two been at it again? I wish you'd make up your minds what your exact relationship is. It's very wearing on the rest of us not knowing.

Bernard enters, a scrap of paper in his hand.

Bernard (*Reading*) For something special. Something from the past. Something with a touch of the old world about it.

Nan Are you all right, Bernard?

Matt He's been drinking.

Bernard (*Reading*) Brown Briar Pipe Tobacco. The flavour of yesterday. No, no, sorry – Yesterday's flavour. How about that?

Matt If you haven't gone insane, Bernard, please enlighten us.

Bernard You remember Andy Mahon?

Matt Not easy to forget. His bandy legs in tights are a permanent blight on the memory.

Bernard His brandy legs don't seem to be a handicap to him these days. He's in advertising now and it was him on the phone. He's doing a TV commercial for Brown Briar Pipe Tobacco.

Matt Never heard of it.

Bernard He wants a well-spoken, distinguished type. And remembered me.

Matt How kind!

Bernard He'd like me to go to Dublin Friday morning to film it.

Nan Yes, of course, go, Bernard. And good luck to you.

Matt We are rehearsing Friday morning.

Nan Take no notice, Bernard, you go. There's probably an early train. If not, there'll be a bus.

Matt I intend to rehearse Friday morning.

Nan (*To Bernard*) But be back in time for the show.

Ted Nan, please, what's the show tomorrow night. I have to know.

Nan We could repeat Jane Eyre.

Ted Who plays Mason? Leonard's gone, remember.

Nan You can.

Ted I'm already the Vicar.

Matt Double it.

Ted I can't. They're on together in the wedding scene.

Nan (*Thinking it out*) We – we could have the wedding offstage – and – and only hear the Vicar's voice. (*Turning to Bernard*) Tell me, Bernard, how come you know the script of that commercial?

Bernard Andy read it to me over the phone so I could work on it. I scribbled it on a scrap of paper in the Post Office. The proper script should be in the post tomorrow.

Matt (*Loudly*) Can we begin?

Nan (*Holding up the letter*) Before we begin could I read this out to you all to see what you think of it?

Matt What is it?

Nan My letter to Billy. I've been writing it in the dressing room.

Ellen What letter?

Nan Of course, Ellen, you weren't here when we talked about it.

Bernard Nan wants to invite the super star to make an appearance with us.

Ted What super star?

Nan Billy. Billy Brien.

Ellen (*Very pleased*) Billy?

Nan Yes.

Ellen (*Getting up*) Would he?

Alec (*Indicating Ellen*) Look at her. She's having an orgasm already.

Bernard (*Looking at his scrap of paper*) For something special. Something from the past. Something with a touch of –

Ellen Oh, shut up, Bernard.

Alec Yes, Bernard, shut up. We're, oh, so dying to hear whether sexy Billy will come or not.

Ellen (*To Alec*) Turn it off.

Ted (*To Alec*) Yes, turn it off.

Alec (*To Ted*) Are you speaking to me?

Nan Now, listen –

Alec (*To Ted*) I said: Are you speaking to me?

Nan Shut up, Alec and listen. Now this is only a rough outline. Dear Billy. How are things? From what we hear, booming, as far as you are concerned. (*Looking up*) This is the hard bit. I want to be straight with him. I want him to understand why we need him to come.

Bernard Because the business is lousy.

Nan Exactly, Bernard, dear. But I don't want to put it so bluntly.

Matt We do not need that jumped-up spear carrier to improve our business.

Nan (*Reading*) We are all well this end, but audiences have been a bit thin of late.

Bernard Thin? Bloody invisible, more like it.

Nan (*Reading*) You did say last time you were down you'd love to do something with us again.

Matt *We* didn't say *we'd* love to do something with *him*.

Nan (*Reading*) Well, here's your chance. Come down and do a play with us. Play a full week on one of our good dates, perhaps. One of your old parts, maybe –

Ellen He's not going to come down just to do one of his old parts.

Ted What *were* his old parts?

Ellen Smallish parts. Second lead parts.

Matt All he was worth.

Nan Listen. (*Reading*) Or pick a nice part for yourself. Something you really want to play – we'll make no objections, as long as we can cast it with our small company.

Bernard Supposing he picks one of *my* parts?

Matt He daren't lay his hands on anything of *mine*. I am, after all, Matthew Monahan. We *are* the Monahan Players. No one touches *my* parts.

Alec *I'm* giving up no parts to accommodate him. Not to accommodate that plastic Romeo.

Ted He can have *my* parts.

Ellen (*To Ted*) Oh, come on, Ted, Billy doesn't want two-bit walk-ons.

Alec (*To Ellen*) Oh, Billy doesn't want two-bit walk-ons. Billy wants big, beautiful, glamorous parts, so you and all you bloody silly bitches can drool, dribble and drawl all over him.

Nan (*Reading*) Anyway, do mull it over and let us know. We're here for the rest of the week and Wicklow next week. Remember all the times you did Wicklow with us?

Matt It was in Wicklow he stuck a wooden spear through my foot.

Nan He didn't stick it through your foot. It only grazed your toe.

Matt Whatever it grazed. It shows what an incompetent, inefficient, useless performer he was.

Bernard (*To himself, looking at the scrap of paper*) *Something* from the past. Something –

Ted Sorry, Bernard?

Bernard Or should it be, d'you think, Something from the *past*? Don't you feel that the emphasis might be on past?

Matt The emphasis might be on forgetting all about the stupid thing. You are letting yourself down doing it – demeaning yourself.

Bernard (*Looking up*) You feel – do you, Matt – from the *past*?

Matt I do *not* feel from the past! I feel very much from the *present*. An actor from the present. Looking towards the future.

Ted He didn't mean that, Mr Monahan.

Matt It's the only proper outlook for an actor. Live in the present. Look to the future.

Ted No, Mr Monahan, Bernard wanted, d'you see –

Matt Live in the present. Look to the future. Till the day you drop.

Nan Please. I want to get this letter off.

Matt Past glories, triumphs, past failures are nothing to an actor. Theory. As if they'd never happened. They have no or little bearing on his work today. On what he's doing now.

Ted Bernard, you meant, didn't you – ?

Matt That's all that matters. What he's doing now. The work today. Laying the groundwork for the future. At ninety an actor must still be laying groundwork for the future. The long, long perfection of his art and craft. The uphill struggle towards that goal. A lifetime's work.

Bernard On the other hand. (*Bernard is looking at his piece of paper*)

Nan On the other hand if Billy doesn't come, if we cannot dredge up something to push the business up – we close. It's as brutal as that.

Bernard (*Looking at his paper*) On the other hand the word to hit could be "from".

Nan No amount of talk about perfecting one's art and craft or about laying groundwork for the future will change that. It'll only be so much hot air if the business remains bad.

Bernard (*Looking at his paper*) Something *from* the past.

Ted Aye, Mr Monahan, there's little use perfecting your craft if there's no one to come and see it.

Matt There's every use. Good Christ, a priest doesn't stop saying Mass because there's an empty church in front of him. Flowers don't stop growing because there's no one to pick or admire them. An actor with talent is a God made creature, who neglects his abilities at his peril. Woe to the man who has to face his maker with none of his natural talents developed. Actor, dancer, painter, fiddle player, your day of reckoning is at hand if you have let go to rust your God given skills. There is nothing more ugly in the sight of God than wasted ability, wasted craft, entrusted to you to create beauty, to enrich in some degree the impoverished souls of the people of this world. It's a mission of the loftiest kind – never forget that. The man who uses his art well sends a shine around the globe, influences men and nations and lights up this dark earth with gay laughter and sweet sights and sounds, with noble thoughts that linger in the air forever.

Pause

Ted Aye, I suppose there's a lot in what you say, Mr Monahan. Still, it'd be nice if we got a full house once in a while.

Pause

Nan (*Reading slowly*) . . . here for the rest of the week. And Wicklow next week. (*Pause*) Love, Nan.

Pause

Bernard Something with a touch of the old world about it. Yes: I think that's it. (*Slowly: deliberately*) Something with a touch of the old world about it.

Nan I'll post off the letter today. Unless anyone wants to suggest changes to it.

Ellen It sounds fine, Nan.

Ted Sounds fine to me too, Nan.

Alec Oh, fine, fine, Nan. We can't wait for raunchy Bill to come!

Nan I'll nip down and post it.

Matt A rehearsal is about to begin.

Nan (*Going*) Won't be a minute.

Bernard Brown Briar – Brown – Brown Briar Pipe Tobacco.

Matt Bernard!

Bernard Yes?

Matt Put a sock in it, dear boy.

Bernard Put what in it?

Ted Yes, Bernard, we're going to rehearse.

Bernard What was it you said, Matt?

Ted (*Giving out scripts*) Script everyone.

Bernard (*To Ted*) What did Matt say to put in it?

Ted (*To Alec*) Script.

Alec snatches the script from Ted.

Bernard (*To Matt*) You want me to put more – (*He makes a wide gesture with his arm*) more – more – you know – in it? Is that it, Matt?

Alec rises, gets the Roman standard, brings it down and hands it to Bernard.

Alec Here. That's what he wants you to put in it.

Bernard The standard?

Ted (*Shouting across to them*) Careful! Careful with that standard.

Bernard (*Holding the standard, he turns to Matt*) What are you talking about, Matt? I can't put a Roman standard in a bloody commercial for pipe tobacco.

Blackout

Scene Four

Tuesday morning. Later. All standing around looking at scripts. Suddenly Matt turns to them.

Matt I've decided. We're doing Caesar tomorrow night instead of Merchant.

Nan Who will play Caesar?

Matt I will.

Ted You're Antony, Mr Monahan.

Matt I will double the parts.

Nan Double them? They'll know it's you.

Matt I will disguise myself.

Nan They'll laugh you off the stage.

Matt Do a different make up for Antony.

Bernard But they're on together, old man.

Matt Not a lot. And only early in the play. Once Caesar is assassinated it's just Antony.

Alec What about when Caesar speaks to Antony?

Ted And Antony addresses Caesar, doesn't he, Mr Monahan?

Alec Then there's the "Let me have men about me that are fat" speech. Caesar actually speaks to Antony by name.

Ted And Antony speaks to Caesar by name, Mr Monahan.

Matt Yes, well, we'll cut the names. Don't be complicated. It's simple. I've been going through it, I'll cut the line: He loves no plays as thou dost, Antony. It'll work.

Nan It won't work. Really, Matt, it's mad doing Caesar like this.

Ellen And I don't like playing Cinna. I feel ridiculous. Everyone knows I'm a woman.

Alec Oh, we all know you're a woman. How could we not, with you eyeing everything that moves in trousers?

Ellen They know it's me. I've always felt extremely uncomfortable doing Cinna.

Matt Lower your voice.

Ellen I get it as low as it will go. It's still a woman's voice.

Matt You're on the programme as Walter Plinge.

Ellen They're still not fooled. And it ruins it for me when I come on as Portia. I feel they want to laugh when I appear as Portia.

Alec We *all* want to laugh when you appear as Portia.

Nan Ellen's right, Matt. It's absurd when we appear as men. No one's taken in. And, as she says, it takes away from our performances later in our proper parts, Calpurnia and Portia.

Matt It shouldn't, it shouldn't, if it's done well.

Nan You can't do that sort of thing well. Not in a million years can I get away with the Soothsayer, no matter how well I do it.

Bernard Lovely part, the Soothsayer. I did it once with Benson in Scotland.

Nan It is a lovely part, Bernard. For a man. But a woman can't do it. And it makes us – well, frankly, it makes us tatty attempting it. We've always tried not to be tatty, and I think succeeded, no matter how bad things were.

Ted Oh, no one says we're tatty, Nan. They always say everything about our shows is miles ahead of all the other companies.

Nan We've always tried to preserve a certain standard.

Ted Sets, costumes, the general level of acting. Everyone says they're first rate, as far as the Monahan Players are concerned.

Nan They do: I know.

Ted And you've never done variety and gag shows like some of them. You've never even had a raffle.

Ellen God preserve us from gag shows. I couldn't do it. I know I couldn't.

Ted Aye, but some of the gaffs knocking around do nothing else. They never work from a script. Gag the whole show.

Ellen We used to call it improvisation at RADA. I was hopeless at it – absolutely hopeless! I need a script.

Ted That lot I was with the summer before last, that Cronin lot.

Nan They've got a terrible name.

Ted Jesus, you should have been with them, Nan. You never saw a script. Or if you did, it was but a flimsy scrap of paper with four or five of your lines scrawled on it. And you got your part and the plot half an hour before the curtain went up.

Ellen You mean they only decided what the play would be half an hour before the curtain?

Ted Sometimes less than half an hour.

Ellen But wouldn't the play be already billed?

Ted Ah, that'd make no difference. There was a play billed for every night of the week and matinees as well, but that was no indication what you were going to do. For instance, Wednesday night was always billed as The Green Trees of My Home.

Bernard Never heard of it.

Ted No one ever had, Bernard. There was no such play. The title pulled them in. I remember doing five different plots under that name. And none of them bore the slightest relation to the title.

Nan But did no one ever query it?

Ted Never in my experience, Nan. Once we gagged a plot about the survivors of an air crash. They got the idea from an air crash in South America the week before. They were always doing that: pinching plots from newspapers and announcing it as the full, authentic story of whatever the incident was. The air crash plot was done under the title The Old Priest Dies.

Bernard There was an old priest on the plane?

Ted There was no mention of a priest, old, young or any age whatsoever. No one bothered to question the title. Like The Green Trees of My Home, The Old Priest Dies brought the punters flocking in. Mrs Cronin read the account of the air crash in the Evening Herald while she was having her tea at six o'clock. She sent the van with the loudspeaker round the town shouting out the news we were doing the full story of the South American air crash. She came to the hall about seven, told us the plot, gave us our parts and the curtain went up at eight.

Ellen It must have been scary.

Ted No one turned a hair. I think it was that night a fellow came round and said to me: And didn't th'oul' priest die great!

Bernard Perceptive gentleman.

Ted Oh, you don't know the half of it, Bernard. But let me tell you something, Nan, it brought the audience in.

Nan Aye, I've heard tell they're near millionaires, the Cronins.

Ted Imagine a big fire in Galway. Six people burnt to death. In all the papers. The Cronins would stage it. You wouldn't get standing room half the time. And if there was a film that everyone was talking about, they'd do the stage version.

Nan Well, please God, we never descend to that.

Ellen Didn't they do variety?

Ted Variety every night. A sketch. And a raffle.

Ellen I wouldn't mind doing variety – I can sing.

Alec *I* can sing.

Ellen You can do comedy, Ted.

Alec *I* can do comedy.

Ellen And, Nan, you can tap. You did it for us once.

Nan Oh, maybe once, not now.

Ellen You know – it might be fun.

Matt We are not doing variety. We are not picking plots out of the Evening Herald. Nor are we having a raffle.

Nan Doing Julius Caesar as we're trying to do it isn't much of a cut above all that, Matt.

Matt I have been waiting all morning to rehearse. My patience is fast running out. I wish to begin. Page eighteen, please. Act Three. The vital scene. We'll work the parts out. All behind me. You, Nan, over there. (*All line up behind Matt R. Nan stands centre. All walk towards her*) Right. The Ides of March are come.

Nan (*In her own voice*) Ay, Caesar. Sorry. (*She lowers her voice*) Ay, Caesar. But not gone. Oh, Matt, this is ridiculous.

Matt (*Ignoring her*) We cut down to Popilius's line.

Ted Popilius? Who the hell's he?

Ellen He's cut.

Matt Popilius is cut. His line is in. Who says it?

Alec I don't say it.

Ellen I don't.

Bernard You say it, Matt.

Nan Matt can't say it, not as Caesar.

Bernard He used to say it as Antony.

Matt Antony isn't in this scene.

Ted He is in the script, Mr Monahan.

Matt Not in this new version. I am Caesar now. So we cut Antony. Someone else must speak Popilius's line.

Nan I can't. Not as the Soothsayer.

Alec I can't as Cassius. I mean the line is addressed to Cassius.

Matt You say it, Ellen.

Ellen I'm Cinna. I can't say: I wish your enterprise today may thrive. Cinna's part of the conspiracy. It's his enterprise as much as the others.

Matt Say the damn line. Stop being complicated.

Ellen (*Sulkily*) I wish your enterprise today may thrive.

Matt And get your voice down. Dammit, you are Cinna, the poet.

Ellen I'm Cinna, the comedian, doing it this way.

Matt The line – please!

Ellen I wish your enterprise today may thrive.

Alec What enterprise, Popilius?

Matt For Christ sake, how many times do I have to say it? There's no Popilius. There was no Popilius the last time we did it.

Bernard We disposed of the bugger.

Alec I am perfectly aware there is no Popilius. I used to say my line to Antony, because it was he who said: I wish your enterprise today may thrive. But now there's no Antony.

Matt Just say: What enterprise? Don't add any name.

Ellen What happens to the next line?

Bernard What *is* the next line?

Ellen Popilius says: Fare you well.

Matt For the last time – there's no blasted Popilius.

Ellen Who says: Fare you well?

Matt You do.

Ellen I can't. I'm not going anywhere. I can't say: Fare you well and not go anywhere. I have a line in a moment.

Matt Go and come back.

Ellen Go where?

Matt (*Points UL*) Over there. Stroll over there.

Ellen Why do I stroll over there?

Nan Yes, she can't stroll over there for no reason.

Alec Why not? She strolls all over the bloody place in every play we do and she never looks as if she has a reason.

Ellen (*Approaching Alec*) I am getting just the slightest bit tired of your continuous smart remarks.

Ted Aye, give it a rest, Alec.

Alec (*To Ted*) Excuse me: did you say something?

Ted It's unfair on Ellen trying to rehearse with you scoring off her all the time.

Alec And what if I do? What is that to you? What happens between her and me has nothing to do with you.

Ted It might have.

Alec It might have? What does 'It might have' mean?

Ted What I said. What happens to Ellen might have something to do with me.

Alec I want that explained.

Matt And I want the rehearsal to proceed.

Alec No, I'm sorry, Matt –

Nan Alec, you mustn't let your personal affairs interfere with your work: it's unprofessional.

Alec No, I'm sorry, I want to know –

Matt Shut up, Alec. (*To Ellen*) Now: say the line.

Ellen What line?

Matt Fare thee well.

Ted Fare *you* well.

Matt (*To Ted*) Not you! Ellen.

Ted I know it's Ellen. I'm saying the line is Fare you well not Fare thee well.

Matt (*To Ellen*) Whatever it bloody is: say it!

Ellen (*Not moving*) Fare you well.

Matt And go.

Ellen (*Pointing to UL*) Over there?

Matt Yes. (*Ellen moves UL*)

Bernard Now in the script it says I say: What said Popilius Lena?

Everyone else Popilius is cut!

Bernard I know the bastard is cut. I'd be grateful if you'd allow me to finish. I used to say: What said Mark Antony?

Nan Antony is cut now too.

Matt Only in this scene.

Bernard Yes, yes, I know. But do I say: What said Cinna?

Matt Why should you say: What said Cinna?

Bernard Because Ellen has taken the line and Ellen is Cinna.

Matt Yes.

Bernard Yes, what?

Matt Yes, say: What said Cinna?

Bernard Ah, but isn't Cinna with us?

Ellen Not at the moment, no. I've strolled over here.

Bernard No, dear. I meant on our side – in the conspiracy.

Matt (*Loud*) Say the bloody line!

Bernard What said Cinna?

Alec He wished today our enterprise might thrive.

I fear our purpose is discovered.

Now that's absurd. Our purpose can't be discovered by Cinna. He knows about it already.

Matt Carry on.

Bernard Do I say: Look, how he makes to Caesar? He's nowhere near Caesar.

Nan Where is Caesar supposed to be? Where are you supposed to be, Matt?

Matt Where I always am in this scene. On the rostrum up centre.

Matt goes UC.

Nan Yes, but Caesar's normally there talking to Antony.

Matt (*A note of exasperation in his voice*) I'll damned well talk to myself then. Carry on.

Bernard Do I say the line or not?

Matt Cut it. Cassius picks it up.

Alec Casca, be sudden, for we fear prevention.

Nan Hold it. Who's Casca?

Ted There's no Casca, Nan. I took all his lines.

Matt Take them again.

Alec I can't remember, did I say: Casca? Or did I just say: Be sudden etc. without mentioning his name.

Matt Just say: Be sudden etc. without mentioning his name.

Alec Be sudden for we fear prevention.
Brutus, what shall be done?

Matt The rest of that speech is cut.

Alec It never used to be.

Matt It is now. Brutus picks it up.

Bernard Do I, by Christ? What do I say? Where are we?

Ted Cassius, be constant.

Bernard Ah. Cassius be constant
Popilius Lena speaks not of our –
Oh, of course. Popilius is gone. Who's taken the bugger's place? I've forgotten.

Ellen I have.

Bernard Who are you? I've forgotten that too.

Ellen Cinna.

Bernard But I can't say –

Matt Yes, you can. Carry on.

Bernard Cinna speaks not of our purposes;
For, look, he smiles and Caesar doth not change.
(*Looks at Ellen*) And is she going to smile? The line's bloody nonsense if she doesn't.

Matt (*To Ellen*) Smile.

Ellen puts on a sarcastic smile, then quickly turns it off again.

Alec Trebonius knows his time, for look you, Brutus,
He draws Mark Antony out of the way.
Used I say that? I never remember us having a Trebonius.

Matt We didn't. You used to say: Antony knows his time. And I used to draw Caesar out of the way.

Ted But why would Antony draw Caesar out of the way, Mr Monahan? In the text Trebonius is doing it because he's carrying out his part in the plot. But there's no reason, as far as I can see, why Antony would do it.

Matt Is this a damned debating society or something? Carry on.

Ted So what will happen now, Mr Monahan?

Matt Cinna can pull me out of the way. (*To Alec*) Say Cinna instead of Trebonius in that speech. Good. Excellent. We' re doing fine. Carry on.

Ellen We can't carry on. The next two lines are cut. And then it's me.

Nan What do you say?

Ellen Casca, you are the first that rears your hand.

Matt There's no Casca. You just say it to Ted.

Alec (*Sarcastically*) Yes, Ted, you are the first that rears your hand.

Nan Shut up, Alec.

Matt (*To Ellen*) What are you waiting for? Say the line to Ted.

Ellen I can't say the line to Ted stuck up here like a cherry on a fruitcake.

Matt Stroll down.

Ellen But I've just been up whispering to Caesar. If I'm part of the plot against him would I have been up whispering to him?

Matt It heightens the sense of intrigue. Rome was a hive of intrigue and conspiracy at the time.

Ellen (*Coming down to Ted*) So – I leave Caesar –

Matt You leave Caesar.

Ellen I leave Caesar. Down I come.

Matt Down you come.

Ellen Down I come. And speak to Ted. Where's Ted?

Ted Right behind you.

Ellen (*Turning*) You are the first that rears your hand.

Ted Am I?

Bernard I'm lost. Where does he say 'Am I?'

Alec He doesn't. Shakespeare never wrote a banal line like 'Am I?'

Ted What do I say? Where are we?

Matt We're at Caesar's line. Are we all ready? I come down. Group yourselves around ready for the murder. Come on, come on, gather round. What is now amiss that Caesar and his senate must redress?

Nan The next line is Metellus. Who's Metellus?

Ted I am. (*Kneeling before Caesar*) Most high, most mighty and most puissant Caesar, Metellus Cimber throws before thy seat an humble heart –

Matt I must prevent thee Cimber –

Nan Can I say something? Last time we did it, I remember Ted was being addressed as Decius Brutus.

Ted Christ, yes, you're right, Nan, I was.

Nan Has he now changed to Metellus?

Matt 's He's Metellus, Decius, Casca – all the smaller male parts.

Alec I know a joke about smaller male parts.

Ted I kneel in front of Caesar like this.

Matt No, not in front. Kneel to one side.

Ted I always knelt in front of Leonard.

Matt Leonard is not playing Caesar now. I am. Kneel to the side.

Ted (*Kneeling L of Matt*) If you say so, Mr Monahan.

Matt I must prevent thee, Cimber. No need to do all this speech now. I cut to the end. Know, Caesar doth not wrong, nor without cause Will he be satisfied.

Pause

Bernard Who has the next line?

Ellen It's Metellus again.

Nan You're Metellus, Ted.

Bernard He's every bloody thing.

Ted Is there no voice more worthy than my own
To sound more sweetly in great Caesar's ear
For the repealing of my banish'd brother?

Bernard (*Trying to move to Matt from the left*) I kiss thy hand – I can't bloody kiss thy hand. I can't get near you, Matt. Is this kneeling effigy going to remain anchored here all day?

(He indicates Ted)

Ted You kissed Leonard's hand from the other side, Bernard.

Bernard I did not kiss his hand from the other side. Always I kissed it from this side.

Nan I think you're mistaken, Bernard.

Alec (*Who is right of Matt*) I remember Bernard was on that side. I was on this side.

Ted Where was I?

Ellen You were in front, Ted.

Ted I was. I *was* in front. I knew I was in front. That's what's caused the shagging complication.

Matt (*Pointing right*) Kneel that side.

Alec He can't kneel this side. He'll be in my way.

Ellen Oh, God, don't anyone please get in Sir Henry Irving's way.

Alec (*To Ellen*) Bitch.

Matt Bernard.

Bernard Yes?

Matt Your speech.

Bernard Mine.

Matt Yes, dear boy.

Bernard Is it, by God? Cassius, be constant –

Ted You've said that.

Nan We're at the bottom of the page, Bernard.

Bernard Yes, but, hold on, hold on. What about Caesar's long speech? You haven't said Caesar's long speech, Matt.

Matt I cut to cue to save time.

Bernard Did you, by Christ? No one told me.

Ted I kiss thy hand. That's where you were, Bernard.

Bernard I kiss thy hand. By Jesus, we were pretty nippy getting down there.

Matt Could we have your speech, please, Bernard.

Bernard I kiss thy hand, but not in flattery, Caesar, desiring that Publius Cimber may have an immediate freedom of repeal.

Ellen Excuse me.

Matt Yes?

Ellen I take it Publius Cimber is Metellus Cimber's brother.

Matt Naturally.

Ted Aye, I've referred to him as the brother.

Ellen (*To R of Matt*) But you're addressed somewhere else as Decius. You can't be Decius and Metellus.

Matt Just refer to him as Metellus.

Ted I'm Metellus then, not Decius?

Matt Yes, yes, Metellus. Now, it's my line. What, Brutus?

Alec Pardon, Caesar, Caesar pardon. Could someone please get out of the effing way. I have to get near Caesar.

Matt (*To Ted, who is standing right of Matt*) Why are you standing there?

Ted You told me to move here, Mr Monahan.

Alec Previously, as befitted a bit player, you moved to behind Caesar.

Ellen I wouldn't let him speak to you like that, Ted.

Matt (*Pointing right*) All right, stand to the side there beyond Alec when you rise.

Ted I'll do that, Mr Monahan. (*Moving RC*) I don't mind doing that at all. But I resent being addressed as a bit player.

Ellen Especially by someone who has had the most minute experience.

Ted Exactly. Especially by someone whose experience is, to be blunt, pretty bloody null and void.

Matt (*Shouting*) Pardon, Caesar, Caesar pardon. Please!

Alec Pardon, Caesar, Caesar pardon. (*He turns to Ted*) Let me tell you I've had experience, good fucking experience. (*He kneels to Matt*) As low as to thy foot doth Cassius fall – (*He turns to Ellen*) And you, you cow, what have you done since they slung you out of RADA? Apart from this, eh? Shag all. Bloody shag all. As low – as low as to thy foot – (*To Ted*) Your tatty gag show company, that's all you know about this business. As – as low as to thy foot doth Cassius – (*To Ted*) And you have the fucking cheek to speak to me like that, you barely qualified bloody stage hand. How dare you speak to me about my experience. You cock up of an amateur. As low as to thy foot doth Cassius fall. To beg enfranchisement for Publius Cimber.

Matt I could be well moved etc., etc. Big speech. I'm cutting. Take note, Bernard, I'm cutting to save time.

Bernard Cutting? Where? Where are you cutting to?

Matt I'm cutting to the –

During the following argument Alec, Ted and Ellen do not move, but argue holding their scripts as if they were still rehearsing.

Ellen (*Laughing, to Alec*) What experience? What experience are you talking about?

Ted (*To Alec*) What have you done, for Jesus sake?

Matt Cutting to the bottom of the big speech, Bernard. That I was constant –

Alec I don't intend to go into what I've done for you bloody no-hopers. A fucking ASM and an over age student.

Matt That I was constant Cimber should be banish'd –

Ted I'm no ASM. I'm stage director and company manager.

Matt – Cimber should be banish'd.

Bernard You've said that.

Ted Isn't that right, Nan? It's in my contract. Isn't that right, Mr Monahan?

Matt – should be banish'd

And constant do remain –

Alec Company manager! That's the first time I've heard we've a company manager.

Ellen I've always known Ted was company manager.

Nan And a very good company manager he is too.

Matt And constant do remain to keep him so.

Nan Quite right, Matt. We've no intention of giving the job to anyone else.

Ellen (*To Alec*) You're extremely jealous. That's the long and short of it. Extremely jealous that Ted, who really doesn't have any ambitions to be an actor –

Alec No one in their right mind would let him within a mile of being a bloody actor.

Ellen (*To Alec*) Yes: jealous! Because Ted should display such talent. That's what upsets you.

Matt Finished my speech. (*Loudly*) I've finished my speech.

Bernard Which speech, Matt? I'm lost again.

Alec (*To Ellen*) Talent? What talent?

Ellen Ted's talent.

Matt Caesar's 'I could be well moved' speech.

Bernard Ah: I've got it.

Matt I've said the cue.

Ellen Ted has shown great ability as an actor.

Alec (*Laughing*) Oh, my Christ.

Nan Please. Matt is trying to finish his speech.

Matt I *have* finished my speech.

Alec Talent? He can't even mend a bloody fuse.

Ellen That's what you can't bear. Not only is Ted a super stage manager –

Matt (*With great emphasis*) That I was constant Cimber should be –

Ted I believe I do a good job.

Matt Should be banish'd. And constant do remain to keep him so.

Nan That's the cue.

Bernard Whose cue?

Matt Cinna's cue.

Nan Your cue, Ellen.

Ellen You do a very good job, Ted. My cue?

Nan Yes.

Ellen What do I say?

Alec (*To Ellen*) He does a very good job messing us all about on stage.

Matt You say: O Caesar –

Ellen (*Very casually*) O Caesar –

Matt Not like that. Put some life into it. You're about to stab him.

Ellen (*Shouting: overdoing it*) O Caesar –

Ted (*To Alec*) I do not mess anyone about.

Matt Hence! Wilt thou lift up Olympus?

Alec (*To Ted*) Oh, no? What about the heavenly choir coming on instead of the car crash in Murder Mistaken?

Matt (*Loudly: deliberately*) Hence! Wilt thou lift up Olympus?

Ellen (*To Alec*) That wasn't Ted's fault.

Alec (*To Ellen*) No, no, it's never his shagging fault.

Matt (*Shouting*) Hence –

Bernard Matt's lifted up Olympus a dozen bloody times. Could someone please answer him?

Alec (*To Ellen*) He's an incompetent frigging amateur.

Ellen (*To Alec*) And you're a disgrace to the profession,

Ted (*To Alec*) Second rate: that's what you are.

Alec (*To Ted*) Tat merchant!

Nan Great Caesar, Ted.

Ted (*Shouting*) Great Caesar. (*To Alec*) I'll break your fucking neck.

Alec You bloody try, mate. You just bloody try.

Matt Doth not Brutus bootless kneel?

Ted (*To Alec*) Think I wouldn't, do you? Think I wouldn't?

Nan Kneel, Bernard. You're supposed to kneel.

Bernard Kneel? I can't even scratch myself in this scrum.

Matt Let Bernard kneel.

Ellen (*To Alec*) You're an arrogant big head.

Alec (*To Ellen*) And you're a brainless, untalented bitch.

Matt Doth not Brutus bootless kneel?

Bernard (*Loudly*) He doth! He's bloody kneeling. And my blasted knee is killing me.

Ted (*To Alec*) Say one word more to her like that, one more word and I'll flatten you.

Matt Casca's line, please! Speak hands for me. You stab Caesar.

The following section should be a fast build-up to Ted hitting Alec.

Nan Ted! Speak hands for me.

Alec (*To Ted*) Amateur.

Ted (*To Alec*) Loud mouth.

Ellen (*To Alec*) Big head.

Matt (*Shouting to Ted*) Speak hands for me.

Nan Ted! Ted! Speak hands for me.

Ted (*Lunging at Alec: shouting*) Speak hands for me!

Alec falls, Ellen screams.

Nan Alec!
Ellen (*Screaming*) You've killed him!

Alec lays stretched on the floor. Nan kneels beside him.

Bernard (To Ted) You've duffed him, by Christ.
Matt (*Turning to Ted*) You fool! I'm Caesar. It's me they bloody assassinate. Not him.

Matt points dramatically at the prostrate Alec.

Blackout

End of Act One

ACT TWO

Scene One. *Thursday morning. Enter Bernard. He carefully places a chair centre and puts a small table beside it. From his pocket he takes a little packet and puts it on the table. He walks away, then walks slowly to the chair, sits, smiles out front.*

Bernard For something special. Something with a touch of the – (*He stops*) Bugger.

He gets up, walks away, then walks back to the chair, sits, smiles again.

For something special. Ah – For something special. Something – yes – something from the past. Something with a touch of the old world about it.

He takes up the packet, holds it up.

Brown Briar Pipe Tobacco. The flavour of – No. No – Yesterday's – yes – yesterday's flavour. (*With emphasis*) Yesterday's flavour.

Nan enters as he finishes. She stands and applauds.

Nan That sounded good.
Bernard Whoever wrote the script of this is in the wrong business. There's an overmuchness of somethings.
Nan Still, darling. It's nice for you to have got it. What time have you to be there tomorrow?
Bernard Eleven. I'm getting the eight o'clock bus to Dublin.
Nan Straight to bed tonight then after the show, so you'll be nice and fresh in the morning.
Bernard I'm nervous as a kitten, love.
Nan (*Laughing*) Go on out of that!
Bernard I've never done anything like this before.
Nan There's always a first time. And you'll be fine.
Bernard I keep forgetting the damn words. Just can't get them right.
Nan I'll hear you. Have you got the script?
Bernard (*Taking the script from his pocket and giving it to Nan*) I walk over to the chair, sit. (*He does this*) For something special.
Nan For something special. That's right.
Bernard I know it's right, I know it's: For something special. Please,

darling, try not to interrupt. It throws my concentration. (*Pause*) What – ah – what comes next?

Nan Something from the past.

Bernard Something from the past. Yes. Something from the past. (*Pause*) Bloody lost again.

Nan Go from the beginning.

Bernard (*Walking away again*) I'm sure I'll never do it.

Nan Of course you will. Now off you go.

Bernard (*Walking to chair*) For something special. Something from the past. (*He sits: pause*) Yes?

Nan Oh, I thought you were pausing.

Bernard No, darling, I was bloody drying.

Nan Something with a touch –

Bernard Yes, yes, I know, I know.

Nan Something –

Bernard Yes, I know, love. You don't have to keep telling me. Something with a touch of the old world about it. (*He takes up the packet. Pause*) I've got the packet. I – hold it up. Got the packet. Hold it up. (*Pause*) What do I say about it?

Nan Let me see. (*Looking at the script*) Oh, yes. Brown Briar Pipe –

Bernard Yes, yes, of course.

Nan – Tobacco. The flavour of yesterday.

Bernard I know, darling. Don' t go on. It breaks the flow. Brown Briar Pipe Tobacco. Yesterday's flavour.

Nan No, dear. The flavour of yesterday.

Bernard (*Loudly*) Yesterday's flavour. Look at the script, darling. You're confusing me.

Nan It's got "The Flavour of Yesterday" written here.

Bernard Oh, Nan, love, do try to get it right. It muddles me to get the wrong prompt.

(*He takes the script from her*)

Nan Well, it muddles me if the wrong line is written in the script.

Bernard (*Looking at the script*) Well, bugger me. I could have sworn it was Yesterday's Flavour.

Nan The Flavour of Yesterday sounds better.

Bernard I'll make an almighty mess of it.

Nan Of course, you won't. You did it very well just now. Tomorrow morning you'll be more fresh. It'll be perfect. You're just right for this.

Bernard It's that damned performance last night. It took it out of me.

Nan It took it out of all of us. Matt was in a state back at the digs.

Bernard We were *all* in a state.

Nan I told him to rest this morning. I hope he will. I want to have a word with you all while he is out of the way.

Bernard I knew it would be a bloody shambles with him doubling Antony and Caesar.

Nan They were giggling, darling. I heard them giggling out front.

Bernard It's a wonder they weren't bursting their sides.

Nan Ever since that disastrous rehearsal on Tuesday –

Bernard When Alec hit the deck?

Nan Yes. Ever since then there's been a blight on the thing. And he still wants to do it for next week's convent matinee.

Bernard No. We must insist, darling. We can't attempt it like that again. They'll run us out of town.

Nan Trouble is we need the convent money. It's the one sure house we can get these days.

Bernard We'll do Shakespeare excerpts. I'm dying to do my Hamlet Ghost again.

Nan You see, that's one of the things I wanted to chat to you all about. Where are the others? Are they coming in this morning?

Bernard I saw Sid and Sue holding hands in that corner cafe on my way down from the digs.

Nan Sid and Sue?

Bernard Ted and Madam Ellen.

Nan God, I hope Alec didn't see them.

Bernard (*Raising his eyes*) Those three!

Nan I never know where I am with them.

Bernard Why did you want Matt out of the way?

Nan Two reasons. I want to discuss what we can do tomorrow night. We can't do Ideal Husband without Leonard.

Bernard There was a time we could repeat a few plays. There was always an audience to see them a second time. And we always had a play or two in reserve.

Nan Those days are gone. Frankly, Bernard, I can't see us going on much longer at this rate. That's really what I wanted to talk over with the rest of you.

Bernard You're not thinking of shutting up shop?

Nan Bernard, love, it's fast coming to that. Matt won't see it. But I'm the one who has to balance the books. Every week we're down. And it has to be made up out of our savings. Having to cough up old Leonard's rent this week hasn't helped either.

Bernard My God, if we close, what do I do about the wife's allowance? Worse: will I have to go back to Poole and live with her?

Nan No, Bernard, you'll be able to pick up some television. I'm sure you will.

Bernard I've never done a part on telly. A real part.

Nan You're doing this commercial tomorrow. If they like it and I'm sure they will – you're bound to pick up a lot more. And it may come in very useful if we have to fold. It could stand you in good stead. You are a good type for television.

Bernard It scares me.

Nan It won't when you've done a few. And if you can't get work over here, I'm sure you will in London.

Bernard Well, anything to keep me from going back to Poole.

Alec comes in. One of his eyes is slightly blackened.

Alec You're going back to Poole, are you, Bernard?

Bernard Not if I can bloody help it, old man.

Nan Morning, Alec.

Alec Morning. Have you recovered yet?

Bernard From last night?

Alec Yes.

Nan Don't mention it!

Bernard I was confused. I couldn't remember whether Matt was Caesar or Antony.

Alec The audience couldn't remember either. You called him Caesar long after he was bumped off.

Bernard He was bloody lucky I called him anything. His double act kept throwing me.

Alec It did. I couldn't get a cue out of you in the tent scene.

Bernard I was muddled, old man.

Alec Do you realize you were using the Roman standard as a walking stick?

Bernard Was I, by God?

Nan I told Ted to take it off you.

Bernard Did he?

Nan Yes.

Bernard Thank Christ for that.

Alec Then the bloody fool didn't know what to do with it.

Nan I kept hissing at him: Hold it up, hold it up.

Alec He was in such a tizzy he kept waving it about like a fairy wand.

Nan And practically decapitated Matt on two occasions. There must be, absolutely must *not* be any repeat of that

Alec I'll refuse to go on. I will. And when I say –

Bernard I just didn't know where I was.

Alec I said half your lines towards the end.

Bernard Thank you, old man.

Alec D'you know, in our version last night Brutus didn't die.

Bernard Didn't he, by Christ?

Alec No, Bernard. You just walked off muttering something about never being so bloody confused in all your life.

Bernard I *was* bloody confused.

Alec So will the audience be when they check the text.

Bernard Perhaps we could say it was a different treatment of the text.

Nan It was that all right!

Bernard They do it all the time in London these days, so I'm told.

Alec And so is the audience told. They know what's going on.

Nan The audience last night didn't know what was going on.

Bernard *I* didn't bloody know what was going on. Matt kept changing wigs.

Alec One for Caesar, one for Antony.

Nan Look: where is Ellen this morning? And Ted? I want to speak to the four of you before Matt gets here.

Alec Ominous.

Nan It is, dear. How is your eye, by the way? It looks better.

Alec Sore still. I'm just waiting my chance to get back at that bastard.

Nan Oh, please, dear, no more fighting. Things are bad enough without that. I was hoping there might have been a letter from Billy this morning. I went to the Post Office full of hope. It's stupid – I realize it – but I was sort of seeing Billy as –

Alec What?

Nan Oh, as – I don't know – a symbol of hope, I suppose.

Bernard You're balmy if you believe Billy jump-up would do anything for us.

Nan No, Bernard, I didn't mean financially. But – I expect it was silly of me – I suppose I clung to the idea that in some vague way Billy would be good for us. He's had his bit of success. We started him and maybe, God knows, I don't know, I hoped some of his good luck might rub off on us. But there's no word from him so far – no letter, no phone call.

Bernard Don't bank on Billy, Nan, my darling. Never bank on the Billys of this world.

Enter Ted and Ellen.

Nan Marvellous. You're here at last.

Ted and Ellen are both obviously ill at ease.

Ted Aye.

Ellen Yes.

Nan Now we're all here, can we gather round? I want to speak to you all.

Ted (*Holding up his hand*) A minute, please, Nan. Ellen and myself –

Nan Yes?

Ted We – we want to speak to you too.

Ellen (*Very nervous*) Yes – yes, we do.

Nan Well, can't it wait, dear? I'm afraid Matt might appear at any moment. I told him to rest. But you know what he's like. And I don't want him here while I'm talking to you.

Ted Won't take a second. Will it, Ellen?

Ellen N – no – no.

Ted We – Ellen and myself – want to let everyone know.

Nan What is it? (*Glancing nervously at Alec*) If it's anything that's going to cause trouble, love, I'd rather not hear it.

Ted No, we hope it won't cause trouble. I don't see why it should cause trouble. We're all grown up people. We should be able to handle it in a mature way

Bernard What the hell are you on about, old boy?

Ted Well – Bernard –

Ellen Y-yes. Yes.

Nan Yes?

Ted Yes. Ellen and I.

Bernard Yes?

Ted Are – engaged.

Bernard Oh, is that all?

Ted We're going to get married.

Bernard That usually follows if you're engaged.

Pause

Ted Well. (*Pause*) That's it. That's what we wanted to tell you.

Nan Oh, congratulations. Yes, yes, congratulations.

Ted Thank you, Nan.

Ellen Thank you, Nan.

Nan I'm sure – (*Glancing at Alec*) I'm sure I speak for us all. I speak for all of us – I'm sure I do – when I say – yes – how pleased we all are.

Bernard Pleased. Yes. Why not?

Ted You – you don't mind, Alec?

Alec Me?

Ted Yes.

Alec (*A little laugh*) Mind? Why should I mind?

Ted Well, we'd like you to wish us luck, wouldn't we, Ellen?

Alec Oh, I do. I do wish you luck. I wish you the very best of luck.

Ellen Thanks, Alec. It's – it's really for the best. It wouldn't have worked with us. You and me, I mean. We were always rowing.

Alec You don't have to explain. You don't have to make excuses. It's nothing to do with me.

Bernard Except you were engaged to her yourself five minutes ago.

Nan Bernard!

Ted I'm really glad you're taking it like this, Alec.

Alec Like what? Taking it like what?

Nan Now, could we, please –

Alec What way should I be taking it?

Ellen As long as – as long as you're not hurt, Alec.

Alex (*Laughing*) Hurt? Hurt? Why in Almighty God's name should I be hurt? (He sits)

Nan Please, folks, I must acquaint you all with the fact that the position of the company is – well, not to put too fine a point on it, dire. Yes, that's the word: dire.

Ellen How do you mean, Nan?

Nan We're losing nearly a hundred pounds every week now.

Sometimes over a hundred. We haven't had a good week for ages. All the losses must be met out of our savings – Matt's and mine. We've never asked anyone to take a salary cut. That's a thing we've never asked.

Alec (*Suddenly jumping up, to Ted and Ellen*) And why you should think, why you should imagine for one minute that I would be upset, pained, put out by the two of you shacking up together, I can't think. No, I can't bloody think. And when I say I can't think, I mean I can't shagging well think.

Bernard We gathered you couldn't, old man.

Nan Well, you can understand that worries me. Having our savings eaten away week after week.

Ellen We don't want you to take it badly, Alec.

Alec Take it badly? I'm not taking it badly. Am I taking it badly? Does anyone observe me taking it badly? No. Of course not. I'm extremely happy about it. Happy in the extreme about the whole business.

(He sits again)

Ted Good.

Nan The fact is – and I want you all to be aware of it – we can't go on like this. And I'm afraid it's come to the point – well, I haven't cleared this with Matt yet, but unless we can come up with some plan or other in the next few days, I'm afraid, yes, indeed, the notice will go up on Saturday. And in a few week's time you'll all be out of a job.

Alec (*Jumping up*) Do you want to know the truth? The real truth? I'll tell you.

Bernard Do.

Alec I am ecstatically glad, over the moon in fact, to be rid of this silly, clinging bitch.

Ellen (*Her hand to her head*) I'm getting a migraine. I know I am.

Ted Watch it, Alec. I won't listen to you speaking about Ellen like that.

Alec You don't have to. Because the subject is closed. Over. Dead. Caput. Yes: cap – bloody – put! I'm rid of her. For ever. About which I'm deliriously ecstatic. (*He sits again*)

Nan So. That's the situation. Unless there's a miracle, the notice will go up Saturday after the performance.

Ted Will Matt agree to it?

Nan Will he have a choice? All the business decisions are made by me. If I make the decision to close he'll have to go along with it.

Ellen We were rather banking on a full summer's work. (*Indicating Ted*) You see, now that we're – we decided we would try to save.

Alec (*Jumping up, speaking to Ellen*) Actually, I have always found you the most boring, absolutely dreary woman I've ever had any contact with. Your persistent moans, your continuous whining, whinging about your aches and pains, your twitches and your stitches, your twinges and spasms. Neurotic: Jesus! That isn't the word to describe you. It's not strong enough. And when I say –

Ted (*Approaching Alec*) You're asking for another thump, mate.

Nan Please. Could we stop this? We are discussing something serious.

Alec (*Sitting again*) Quite right, Nan. Quite right. (*Indicating Ellen*) That excuse for a woman is not in the least bit serious.

Nan The other thing I wanted to discuss is what do we do tomorrow night.

Ted Ideal Husband is billed.

Nan We can't do Ideal Husband without Leonard.

Ted We've nothing else.

Bernard Matt wants to repeat Julius Caesar for the convent matinee next week.

Ellen and Ted No. No. Out. That's out.

Ellen We can't have a repeat of last night. (*Hand to head*) Oh, God, my head! I couldn't face it.

Bernard How about Shakespeare extracts for tomorrow night?

Nan No good, dear. Extracts at night are death.

Bernard Everything at night is death at the moment, darling.

Ted I've just had a – (*He stops*) No, I don't suppose –

Nan What?

Ted You'd never consider it.

Bernard What, old boy? Spit it out.

Ted Well. It could be a quick way – a quick way of getting a show ready in a short time.

Ellen What would?

Bernard What in Christ name are you on about?

Alec (*Still sitting*) I know what he's on about.

Bernard It's more than I bloody do.

Alec He wants us to do a gag show.

Nan (*To Ted*) You don't, surely?

Bernard I couldn't do it, old man. Not at my advanced age.

Ted Well, it was just a suggestion.

Alec (*To Ted*) You're not in a tat outfit now, you know.

Ted I thought it could maybe be a way out for tomorrow night.

Ellen You know – it might be fun.

Bernard Fun? Bloody funny idea of fun!

Ellen Well, we've never tried it.

Bernard I do not wish to, ta all the same.

Nan Oh, we could never do it.

Bernard Never.

Nan Could we?

Alec 'Course we couldn't. Never. And when I say –

Ellen Why don't we try? It might be –

Bernard What?

Ellen Stimulating. Yes. It might be – this pain in my head! – it might be stimulating.

Ted It would mean we'd have a show for tomorrow. A new show. At least we'd get a few more people in than if we did a repeat.

Nan But what could we do, Ted?

Ellen We could think up a plot.

Nan I couldn't think up a plot.

Bernard Thinking up a plot is the job of a writer. We're not writers. We're actors. Every man should stick to his last.

Alec I refuse to have anything to do with it.

Ellen Why? Don't you think you're a good enough actor?

Alec (*Jumping up*) I'm *too* good an actor for that sort of tatty stuff, you malicious cow.

Ted Better actors than you'll ever be, mate, have done gag shows.

Ellen The Commedia Dell'arte was based on improvisation.

Ted It has an honourable tradition in the theatre.

Nan Yes, but, dear, what could we do?

Alec I am not taking part in a phoney replay of a Galway fire!

Ellen Couldn't – couldn't we do the plot of some play we know?

Ted Or some play we've seen.

Ellen Yes: a play we've seen.

Nan It would have to be a small cast.

Ted How about Matt? Would he agree to it?

Nan Never. If we do it, we'll have to keep the whole thing secret from him.

Bernard And how do you propose to do that, pray?

Ted Maybe he could think it was his night off show we're doing.

Ellen Yes, Gaslight is his night off. He could think we're repeating Gaslight tomorrow.

Bernard Excuse me if I appear stupid, dear girl, but Matt will easily discover it's not Gaslight when he glances onstage or when he hears the lines – if we manage to utter any.

Ellen Couldn't we tell him to stay at his digs to rest?

Nan It's true: he does need to rest.

Bernard Would he, darling?

Nan I could be very firm about it. And hope he'd take notice.

Ted (*Walking around, trying to figure out what to do*) What could we do? Get your thinking cap on, Bernard.

Bernard I'm blank, old boy. This isn't my particular wicket.

Ellen Hey! There was that thriller I saw in the West End last summer. That had a small cast. I saw it with Alec. Breakup I think it was called.

Alec Breakdown.

Ellen Breakdown, that's right. We went to that little coffee bar afterwards. Do you remember, Alec? All those lovely candles in bottles. That was a super thriller. Alec raved about it. (*To Alec*) You raved about it.

Bernard You raved about it, did you, old boy?

Nan What was the plot?

Ted (*To Ellen*) Are you sure this is the one you want to do?

Ellen It was a super plot. Wasn't it, Alec? There was – there was –

Alec This fellow, a famous writer, thinks he's having a breakdown. Things happen, but afterwards everyone around him denies they happened. For instance, his mistress calls on him, but later she denies it. She says she never called. He begins to think it's all in his imagination.

Ellen You see, the whole thing is a plot got up by his wife and the mistress.

Alec And the wife's boyfriend.

Ted Complicated.

Bernard Complicated.

Ellen Then there was a police inspector.

Alec A friend of the husband.

Ellen Of the husband, that's right. Not of the wife.

Nan Not of the wife?

Ellen Of the husband.

Bernard Bloody complicated.

Alec He unravels the whole thing.

Ted Who does?

Ellen The inspector, of course.

Bernard Sounds as if it needs unravelling.

Nan What – what does he unravel?

Alec The plot against the husband. They tried to persuade him he was going mad.

Bernard That shouldn't have been hard. With that plot.

Ellen To get his money. To get the husband's money. You see, he was a – (*To Alec*) What was he?

Alec A best selling author.

Nan Would it work?

Ted Could we cast it?

Ellen Let's see. There's the wife, her lover, the girlfriend, the author and his friend the detective.

Alec Three men, two women.

Ellen Perfect for us. Oh, yes, the more I think about it the more exciting the idea becomes.

Nan A pity we couldn't get hold of a script.

Ted There wouldn't be time, Nan. We need it for tomorrow.

Ellen Bernard, you'd be ideal for the inspector.

Alec Bernard, the inspector. Me, the author. (*To Ted*) I suppose we'd have to make do with you as the lover.

Ellen Ted would be perfect as the lover! Although he would be good as the author too.

Alec The author? That spud-yokel as the author? If he's the author, I'm out. And when I say out, I mean (*Spelling*) O – U – T!

Ted Ah, I don't mind what I play.

Ellen There speaks the true pro!

Nan What could *I* do?

Ellen There's the wife and the girlfriend.

Alec You'd be right for the wife, Nan. It's the better part too. We couldn't leave it to the RADA student. (*He indicates Ellen*)

Ted Good, begod, it's cast. All we need do now is to go on and play it tomorrow night.

Nan Don't we need a rehearsal?

Ted Yerra, no, Nan. A rehearsal'd take the freshness away.

Bernard I'm glad it will be fresh, because I doubt it will be anything else.

Ellen (*To Bernard*) It's your commercial tomorrow, Bernard, isn't it? Will you be back from Dublin in time?

Bernard Oh, I should think plenty of time, darling. I'd have had to be back in time for Ideal Husband anyway.

Ted What we need to do is sit down and discuss the plot. So that we know it in detail. But don't act it. Don't even try out scenes. Keep all that for tomorrow night.

Nan But how would we – you know – get into it? How does it begin?

Alec You and me, Nan – the author and his wife. She's going out. She wants to leave me on my own so that her boyfriend can call. Later of course the boyfriend denies he ever called.

Nan Yes, but what do we talk about? You must give me some clue.

Ellen You pretend you have to go out somewhere. Shopping, perhaps.

Nan But I must have an opening line. I've never worked before without a script. I must have something to start me off. I might be all right after that. But I'm lost if I haven't an opening line.

Bernard Try: How in Christ name am I going to get through this bloody thing?

Ted Now, Bernard, oul' son, you're not being helpful.

Ellen Let's think of an opening line for Nan.

Ted Aye, aye, an opening line for Nan. Let's think.

Alec (*Suddenly snapping his fingers*) I've got it!

Nan What?

Alec The perfect opening line.

Ellen What is it?

Alec Perfect. Listen.

(*Enter Tim*)

Tim Did any of ye see an oul' brush I left behind me here last night?

Blackout

Scene Two. *Friday night. An interval during the performance. A very simple box set has been erected with chairs, a sofa, a drinks table. The characters are sitting and standing around, drinking coffee and touching up their make up. They speak quietly, aware that the audience is out front. Long pause.*

Nan Well? What do you think?

Ted Not too bad.

Ellen Not bad at all. They've got the story.

Bernard It's more than I've done.

Ellen You haven't been on yet, Bernard. You'll be O.K. once you're on.

Alec We went haywire on the plot a few times. (*Indicates Ted*) It's this fellow's fault.

Ellen Yes, Ted, you got it wrong. You are not two characters. You're the same person both times.

Ted But if I'm the same guy it messes up the plot.

Alec No, you bloody eejit, that's the whole point. You come first as the fan of mine, who admires my books. Then on your second visit you deny you've been here on your first visit. It makes me think I'm going mad.

Bernard I'm sorry to hear that, old boy. I knew we should never have attempted this.

Ellen You see how I managed it, Ted. I came on my first visit. That scene went very well, by the way, Alec.

Alec Super.

Ellen Then on my second visit I denied I'd ever been here.

Bernard Excuse me, how many visits do I have? I don't really feel I can cope with more than one. As a matter of fact, I don't feel I can cope even with that.

Nan Was *I* all right?

Alec Splendid.

Nan I forgot to say you were going round the bend.

Ellen I said it for you, Nan.

Bernard I'll be going round the blasted bend by the end of the night.

Nan It's not bad once you get started, Bernard. In fact, it's a bit of gas.

Ted (*Slightly sulky*) I've done gag shows before. And I know when I've done all right or not.

Bernard Would someone please fill me in again. I'm hazy about where I fit in.

Alec You're the detective. An old friend of the author.

Bernard (*Pointing to Alec*) You.

Alec Me. I've already rung you asking you for advice.

Bernard About what?

Ellen About helping to clear up the mysterious happenings.

Bernard Which were – let me see now – that she (*Indicates Ellen*) called round and he (*Indicates Ted*) called round, but both denied they had.

Alec Now the crucial thing, Bernard –

Ted (*Still sulky*) I felt my performance was actually quite good.

Alec The crucial thing is that you notice something about Ted, Ellen and Nan.

Nan Matson, Jane and Betty. Let Bernard get used to the characters' names.

Bernard What do I notice? What? Please tell me. Oh, it's all too much in one day. Rushing up to Dublin. Doing that commercial.

Ellen How did it go, Bernard? I forgot to ask.

Bernard Fine. But it's too bloody much. Rushing back. Rushing here. Doing this. First time I've ever done it. Too bloody much. What – what do I notice?

Nan Alec, tell Bernard the important thing.

Bernard (*To Alec*) Yes, for Christ sake, old man, do, please, tell me the important thing.

Ted The important thing is that Jane, Betty and Matson –

Bernard (*Pointing to Ellen, Nan and Ted*) You, you and you.

Ted Right; they're never supposed to have met before.

Alec I told him that.

Bernard Did you, old boy? I don't remember you telling me that.

Nan Yes, Bernard, we three pretend never to have met before.

Bernard Oh, you're only pretending?

Alec Well, of course they're only pretending. The whole thing is set up by them. Don't you get that, Bernard?

Bernard No, old man, I rather think I don't.

Nan Yes, it's part of our plan against Alec. Now when I ask everyone if they'll have a drink – correct me if I'm wrong, Alec – the Inspector –

Bernard Me?

Alec You.

Nan The Inspector is the only one I ask what he will have.

Alec (*To Bernard*) She pours whisky out for Matson and nothing for Jane, but she hasn't asked them what they'll have.

Ellen Thus giving the game away that she knows about their drinking habits and therefore knows them well.

Ted (*To Bernard*) You pounce on that.

Bernard (*To himself*) I pounce on that, I pounce on that.

Ted We'd better be getting ready for the last scene. They've had two long intervals.

They move about, putting away coffee cups: those who are sitting stand.

Alec Now, Bernard, wait for me to say I think I've had a breakdown. Wait for that, then ring the doorbell.

Ted Stand by. I'll kill the house lights, then take the curtain up.

Alec (*To Ted*) You're supposed to be on, you moron.

Ted I know I am, you bloody fool. But I had to go off at the end of the act to bring the tabs down.

Alec I didn't notice you going off. They'll wonder why you went off. You should have invented an excuse.

Nan He did. He said he was going out to have a look through the kitchen window.

Alec Why was he supposed to be having a look through the kitchen window?

Ellen To see if it was going to rain. That's what you said, Ted.

Ted I couldn't think of anything else to say. I had to bring down the tabs.

Alec You've never been in the flat before, yet you know where the kitchen is. Bloody great!

Nan Yes, but – couldn't that be another give away? The audience will think: Ah, how did he know where the kitchen was?

Ellen When you come back on, Ted, you'll have to tell us whether it is going to rain or not.

Ted O.K. (*Going off*) Stand by. I'm taking down the house lights. Stand by, Bernard.

Bernard (*Poking his head round the scenery*) I'm here. Could you tell me again – when do I ring the doorbell?

Alec After my speech saying I think I've imagined it all.

Nan I hope Matt doesn't decide to come down to the hall.

Ellen I thought he was staying at the digs.

Nan I hope he will. I left him with David Copperfield.

Ellen With who?

Nan His favourite novel. He rereads it about every two years. I told him he had to rest and –

Ted (*Off*) Stand by.

Nan (*Whispering*) – ordered him to have an early night.

Ted (*Off*) We're going up.

> *There can be an inner curtain in front of the box set, which now comes across slowly as the actors get to their places. After a pause it opens again. Alternatively, the stage curtain comes down slowly as the actors get to their places. A pause. The house lights come up for a moment, then go slowly down again. The curtain rises. Ellen, Alec and Nan are sitting. During the scene the loud stage whispers (LSW) must clearly be heard by the real audience, but they are intended only for the actors onstage. When they speak the dialogue in the gag-show they should over perform, without losing total reality.*

Alec Well, I can't explain it. How could I have imagined Jane and Matson coming here this morning?

Ellen By the way, where is he?

Nan Matson? He said he was – Now what exactly *did* he say he was going to do?

Ellen Ah – I remember! He said he was going into the kitchen to look out the window.

Alec But if he had never been here before, how could he know where the kitchen was?

Ellen You told him, Betty.

Nan Did I?

Ellen Yes.

Nan Of course I did. Yes, I remember saying: That's the kitchen there. Yes, I remember saying that.

Alec Why couldn't he look out of one of the windows in this room?

Ellen (*Stumped for a moment*) I don't know why. Do you know why, Betty?

Nan No, no, I don't know why.

Ellen (*To Alec*) I wish you wouldn't ask such awkward questions.

Nan Perhaps – yes, that's it, I'm sure – perhaps he doesn't like the windows in this room.

Alec What's wrong with the windows in this room?

Ellen That's it, Betty. He doesn't like the windows in this room. And he said he wanted to see if it was going to rain. Well, I'm sure it's easier to see if it's going to rain from the kitchen window than from any of these windows.

Alec (*Smiling maliciously*) Why?

Ellen (*Gritting her teeth*) Why? I'm – I'm not exactly sure why. But I expect Matson himself knows why.

Nan Yes, we can ask him when he comes back.

Long pause

Alec If he ever *does* come back.

Ellen Shall I call him?

Nan You'd better.

Ellen I just – I just want to make sure he's all right. (*Goes to side*) Are you all right?

Bernard (*Off*) Yes, of course I'm all right. I'm not on yet, am I?

Ellen turns, shocked, stuck for words.

Nan (*Laughing in a forced manner*) There he goes! Putting on his funny voices again. I always said Matson was a joker.

Alec Did you? But you don't know him. You said you'd never met him before today. (*LSW*) You're not supposed to have ever met him before!

Nan (*Laughing louder*) Of course I'd never met him before! Of course I hadn't! But I feel somehow – in the – in the few hours I've known him today that – that I've known him for years. Do you know what I mean? But of course I haven't known him for years. I've never met him before today. I wish that clearly to be understood. I've never met him before today!

Ellen (*Looking off*) I think he must have passed out. (*To Nan*) Do you think he's passed out? (*LSW*) He's holding the whole thing up.

Nan Call him again.

Ellen Are you all right? (*Calling off*)

Ted (*Off in a LSW*) The main switch is banjaxed.

Ellen (*LSW To Nan*) The main switch is broken.

Alec (*Loudly*) Oh, good. I'm glad he's all right. Very pleased he hasn't passed out.

Nan (*Loudly*) Yes, that's good news, isn't it? (*LSW*) Tell him to leave it.

Ellen (*LSW*) Leave it.

Ted (*Off in a LSW*) I can't. The frigging lights will go.

Alec (*Playing for time*) Well, well, well. What a marvellous view there must be from the kitchen window to detain him.

Nan There *is* a marvellous view. You know that as well as I do – it's *our* flat, don't forget.

Alec Who said anything about me forgetting it was our flat? I've always said that view from the kitchen window was – was better than the view – the view –

Nan Of the Bay of Naples.

Ellen The Bay of Naples? What's the Bay of Naples got to do with anything? (*LSW*) The Bay of Naples? Where does that come into the plot?

Ted (*Off: LSW*) I'll have it fixed in a minute.

Ellen (*LSW: To Ted*) Hurry up, for God's sake. (*Loudly*) Yes, he says it doesn't look like rain. Isn't that marvellous?

Nan Marvellous. Marvellous. (To Alec) Isn't that marvellous, John?

Alec John? Who's John?

Nan (*LSW*) I thought you were John.

Alec (*LSW*) Ben. (*Loudly*) Oh, John! You haven't used that old pet name for me in years. John! It's good to hear you calling me that again.

The lights flicker, then come right again. Ellen gives a little scream.

Nan The lights – I think there must be lightning about.

Alec But she said he said it didn't look like rain.

Ellen Ah – but – he – he didn't say it didn't look like lightning.

Lights flicker again.

Nan Oh, my God.

The doorbell rings.

Alec Oh, no.

Ellen (*LSW*) He's too early. (*LSW to Bernard off*) You're too early, Bernard.

Bernard (*LSW Off*) What? What did you say? I can't hear you.

Nan Who is it? Who's at the door?

Alec I'll see.

Alec goes to the door, opens it, calls off.

No, no, we don't want any extra milk today, thank you.

Bernard (*Off: loudly*) What? What the hell are you – ? Who said anything about milk?

Alec (*Closing the door*) It was only the milkman.

Ellen Don't you think we'd better get back to your breakdown?

Alec My breakdown? Yes, yes, I think I must have had a –

Doorbell rings.

(*LSW*) Bloody hell. He's far too early. I'm just starting the speech. (*Loudly*) It's probably the milkman again. (*Alec goes to door, opens it, calls out*) Hello. No, I'm sorry, he doesn't live here. (*He closes the door*)

Bernard (*Off: loudly*) Who doesn't live here? Do you want me bloody on or not?

Alec He'd got the wrong address.

Enter Ted.

Ted That's better.

Ellen What is?

Ted It's fixed.

Nan What's fixed?

Ted Ah – it's fixed – that – that it's not going to rain. I – I was looking through the window – the kitchen window – and I saw straight away it wasn't going to rain.

Alec Could I please continue what I was saying?

Nan Yes – do.

Alec Well –

Ellen Yes?

Alec Well – oddly enough – I can't remember what I was saying,

Ellen About your breakdown.

Alec That's right – my breakdown. I think I must have imagined the whole thing. So I really think I'm going through a – a breakdown.

Pause. Alec calls off loudly.

I said I really think I'm having a breakdown.

Ellen (*After waiting a moment, she walks to the door, calls off*) You said you really think you're having a breakdown, did you?

Nan (*Calling loudly*) Yes, I'm glad you've admitted it. I'm very glad you've admitted you're (*Calling louder*) having a breakdown!

Alec (*LSW*) Where the hell is he?

Ellen (*LSW*) Bernard! The doorbell!

Ted D'you think I should nip off again – nip into the kitchen, that is, to see – well, you know, to see –

Nan To see again if it's going to rain. Yes, good idea. Because – because it looks to me to be clouding over. (To Ted) Have a look through the kitchen window.

Ted goes off.

Ellen (*Walking downstage*) Isn't it marvellous that we have the window in the kitchen.

Alec Why is it marvellous that we have the window in the kitchen?

Ellen (*Turning to Alec, annoyed*) Why? Why? Why do you think?

Nan Oh, *I* think it's marvellous we have the window in the kitchen. I really do. I mean, if we didn't, we wouldn't know – would we? – if – if it was going to rain or not.

Doorbell rings.

Alec Good. (*Rushes to door, opens it*) Ah, George, we've been waiting for you. (*LSW*) Where were you?

Bernard (*LSW*) Every time I rang the bloody bell you shut the door in my face.

Nan And who is this gentleman?

Alec (*Bringing Bernard in*) This is George.

Nan Hello, George.

Ted (*Coming in*) No, it's definitely not going to rain.

Bernard (*To Ted*) What? It's not what?

Ted I've been checking through the kitchen window.

Bernard (*LSW To Alec*) What the hell's he on about?

Alec Now, George is an Inspector at Scotland Yard. He and I are old friends.

Lights flicker on and off.

Ted Not again!

Bernard What's wrong?

Nan It's the lightning.

Bernard Lightning?

Lights flicker again.

Ted Damn. I'll have to go and –

Nan Yes, yes, you go and –

Ellen And – and – and have a look through the kitchen window. You'll see the lightning better from there. (*Ted goes out*)

Bernard (*LSW*) Lightning? Was I supposed to say something about lightning?

Alec (*Loudly*) No, George, you see, none of us knew anything about the lightning.

Bernard (*To Alec*) Could we discuss these strange happenings you rang me about. These strange visits you've been having, old boy. I'm right – am I not? – in saying you've been having strange visits?

Nan Oh, yes, quite right.

Alec No, not quite right.

Bernard No? (*LSW*) I knew I'd get the bloody thing wrong.

Alec Well, you see, George, I think I may have imagined it all. (*To*

Nan and Ellen) You've been telling me all morning I've imagined it all.

Bernard (*To Alec*) You've imagined it all?

Alec I seem to have, George.

Bernard I see. (*LSW*) No, I bloody don't. Where do we go from here?

Ted (*LSW Off*) Could someone give me a hand?

Bernard (*Turning suddenly*) What? What was that?

Ellen I think Matson wants someone in the kitchen.

Alec Yes, he probably wants one of us to look through the window with him.

Bernard What window?

Alec Our lovely window in the kitchen where the view is like the Bay of Naples.

Bernard (*LSW*) For Christ sake, what are you talking about?

Nan I'll go. I expect he'd like some advice about whether it's going to rain or not. (*She goes out*)

Bernard (*LSW*) Where's she gone?

Alec Well, it's very good of you to come round, George. To – to help sort out all this.

Bernard I wish you *would* let me sort it out. (*LSW*) When is she going to pour the drinks? She's supposed to pour the drinks.

Nan screams offstage. All lights go off, then come on again.

Ellen It's – ah – the lightning. I'd better go and see if she's all right. (*Ellen goes out*)

Bernard They're all disappearing.

Alec It's the lightning, George. It's worrying.

Bernard When you phoned me you said nothing about lightning.

Alec You see, George, I imagined this Matson guy called earlier to see me pretending to be a great fan of mine. Then he returned wanting to buy a picture I'm selling and he denied he had ever been here. He said it was his first time to visit my flat. The same thing happened with Jane.

Nan rushes on, crosses the stage

Nan Excuse me a moment. (*She goes out*)

Bernard (*Turning: confused*) Was that – ? Who was that?

Alec That's my wife Betty, George.

Bernard Your wife Betty George?

Alec Yes.

Bernard Why's she running round the place?

Nan returns, crosses the stage holding up a screwdriver.

Nan This is what we need. (*She goes out*)

Bernard What's she doing with a screwdriver?

Alec I expect they need it to fix that window in the kitchen. That's decent of Matson to fix it for me.

Bernard (*LSW*) What do I say now?

Alec How – how are your geraniums, George?

Bernard Geraniums?

Alec Yes, you're a keen geranium grower, aren't you?

Bernard (*LSW*) First I've bloody heard of it. (*Louder*) Am I?

Alec Oh, very. I remember you telling me last time we met that you have a passion for geraniums.

Ellen comes in.

Ellen Everything's all right now. We – we saw the lightning through the window.

Bernard What was the screwdriver for?

Ellen The screwdriver? Oh, that was for – that was for –

Alec For the window. To fix the window.

Nan (*Coming in*) We fixed the table leg.

Bernard Table leg?

Nan That was why we needed the screwdriver. To fix that wonky table leg.

Alec Oh, I thought it was the window.

Ted (*Coming in holding the screwdriver*) I don't think we'll have any more trouble now.

Bernard The table leg's fixed is it, old boy?

Ted Table leg? What table leg?

Alec Ah – yes – yes – now – do you feel like a drink, George?

Bernard Yes, oh, yes, I could do with a drink.

Alec Betty, could you give us all a drink?

Nan Yes, of course. I should have offered you all one ages ago.

Bernard (*LSW*) Yes, you damned well should.

Nan pours drinks.

Alec Betty, haven't you forgotten one little thing?

Nan Have I?

Alec Don't you think you should ask the Inspector what he'd like?

Nan Of course, of course. What would you like, Inspector?

Bernard Whisky, please. (*LSW to Alec*) Is it all right to say whisky?

Slight flicker of lights.

Ellen Oh, I hope those lights – I – I hope there's going to be no more lightning. (*LSW to Ted*) I thought you said you'd fixed it.

Ted (*LSW*) I would have if you'd been any use.

Ellen (*LSW*) You told me to hold the wrong wire.

Ted (*LSW*) I told you to hold the right wire. You held it in the wrong hand.

Bernard What are you two on about?

Alec I do believe they're discussing the lightning, George.

Nan gives drinks to Bernard, Ted and Alec. From all: cheers, good luck etc. They drink.

Alec So.
Ellen Yes.
Nan Yes.
Ted That's the way it goes.
Alec Definitely.
Ellen Yes.
Alec Oh, yes.

Pause

Ted (*LSW*) The drinks, Bernard.
Bernard What?
Alec (*LSW To Bernard*) You noticed about the drinks.
Bernard (*Confused*) Did I? The – the drinks?
Nan (*Very deliberately*) What – about – the – drinks?

They all turn to Bernard.

Bernard The – the drinks? (*LSW*) What about the bloody drinks? It's gone completely.
Nan The drinks? Was there something peculiar about the drinks?
Bernard Was there? (LSW) Was there?
Nan (*LSW To Alec*) You do the drinks speech. *You* could have noticed.
Alec (*Loudly*) Ah! I noticed something.
Ted What did you notice?
Ellen What did you notice?
Ted (*LSW To Ellen*) Think of your own lines. Don't keep repeating me.
Ellen (*LSW To Ted*) It's O.K. to repeat. Sounds realistic.
Alec (*To Nan*) Yes, yes, I noticed.
Bernard Tell us, for God's sake, what you noticed.
Alec I noticed you asked George what he'd have to drink. But you didn't ask (*Indicates Ellen and Ted*) these two.
Bernard (*Suddenly remembering*) Ah! That's right. That's correct. You didn't ask these two. (*LSW To Alec*) I've got it now, old boy. (*Loudly*) But you *did* ask me.
Nan Yes, I did. So what?
Bernard So what? So what? Do not so what me, madam! You thought you were being clever. But you're not so clever. Because what this means is – it means – all this means – (*To Alec*) What *does* it mean?
Alec It means –
Bernard Yes, yes, it means – (*Stops: he turns to Alec*) Well, go on, tell her what it means.
Alec It means you already knew Jane and Matson.
Bernard You did, you did.
Alec You gave Matson a whisky without asking what he'd like. And you didn't give Jane a drink. Because you must have already known she didn't drink.

Bernard (*As if he'd worked it out himself*) Of course! So from that I conclude – I conclude – ah –

Alec You conclude, George, that these three hatched an evil conspiracy against me.

Bernard I do, oh, I do indeed. And I've got some men outside –

Ellen (*Surprised*) Have you?

Bernard I have, madam, I certainly have. And they will take care of all three of you.

Alec Thank you for unravelling that, George.

Bernard Not at all, old man. (*LSW*) I thought I did rather well.

Matt strides through the door looking at a script.

Matt About the convent matinee next week. I thought if we cut Decius Brutus – (*He looks up, stares out front*) Good God!

Ellen Hello.

Nan Yes, hello.

Matt The curtain's up!

Alec Oh, yes, nice curtains up in all parts of the flat.

Bernard (*To Matt*) And who are you supposed to be?

Matt (*LSW*) I thought it was the interval. I heard your voices and couldn't recognize it as a Gaslight scene. So I assumed –

Ellen Who is he?

Ted He's – (*Gives up, unable to come up with an idea*)

Ellen (*To Ted*) Who?

Ted (*LSW To Ellen*) Try and think who, you stupid cow.

Ellen (*Loudly*) Do not call me a stupid cow.

Matt (*Turning to Ellen*) I beg your pardon?

Nan Yes, yes, we must discover who this strange man is.

Matt What strange man?

Bernard (*To Matt*) You, old boy.

Matt I don't understand. Look, could someone please –

Ellen (*To Ted*) You have been extremely objectionable to me all night.

Alec (*Suddenly loudly*) I know who he is.

Ellen Who?

Nan Thank God, someone knows.

Alec (*To Bernard*) He's one of your men.

Bernard Is he?

Alec Yes, the men you referred to just now. One of your juniors.

Matt Juniors?

Alec Oh, I know normally he'd be in uniform. But. I expect he's in plain clothes because – ah –

Ted Because he didn't want to give the game away.

Ellen (*To Ted*) Give what game away? Finish your sentences.

Ted (*To Ellen*) Don't bug me.

Nan Well, I'm glad we've solved that. (*To Matt*) Now we know who you are.

Matt You do?

Alec Yes, you're a plain clothes policeman come to take these three away. (*Indicates Ellen, Nan and Ted*)

Matt (*LSW*) Would someone please explain to me –

Alec Yes, Constable, these three are the villains of the piece. You're here to arrest them.

Matt (*LSW to Bernard*) What *is* this play?

Bernard (*LSW*) Buggered if I know.

Ted I admit my guilt.

Alec He admits his guilt. Did you hear that, Inspector?

Ted (*LSW To Ellen*) And let me tell you I've had it up to here with you. I'm sick of your whining and your moaning

Ellen (*Loudly*) And let me tell *you* something. I wouldn't marry you if you were the only thing in trousers this side of the Irish Sea.

Nan Marry? (*To Ellen*) But you're not thinking of marrying him, Jane? (*LSW*) There's nothing between Matson and Jane.

Ted (*Loudly*) Good. Terrific. As far as I'm concerned it's off.

Matt Off? I don't understand. (*To Alec*) I thought it was *you* she was breaking off with.

Nan But this is the most amazing revelation. To think there was something between Matson and Jane. (*LSW to Ellen*) You're confusing the audience.

Bernard (*LSW*) You're confusing *me*, never mind the bloody audience.

Ted (*To Ellen*) Bitch.

Ellen (*To Ted*) Lout.

Nan Please!

Tim shuffles on mumbling to himself and scratching his head.

Tim I still haven't found that oul' brush.

Nan Oh, God!

Bernard (*To Tim*) And who are *you* supposed to be?

Alec (*Desperate*) Oh, he's – he's – (*Gives up*)

Tim I put it down over there to light a fag, I'm certain I did.

Nan (*Begging Alec to come up with a suggestion*) Who *could* he be?

Alec Ah – I know!

Nan You do?

Alec Yes. (To Bernard) He's your other man. You said you had men outside who would arrest these three. Well, he's one man (*Points to Matt*) and he's the other. (*Points to Tim*)

Nan Of course. He's the second policeman come to take us away.

Tim (*Suddenly looking up at the audience*) Holy God, there's people out there.

Alec (*To Bernard*) Well, come on, get your men to take them to the police station.

Tim The police station? God Almighty, what sort of trouble are we in?

Bernard (*To Matt*) Yes, we'd better get these villains locked up.

Tim All I was doing was looking for th' oul' brush. A fellow outside said the show was over. I thought ye were all sitting around talking.

Nan Sitting around talking, yes, that's right. But now the time has come, you have to take us away.

Tim Have I, ma'am?

Alec You have. You see, they got together to try to persuade me I was mad.

Tim Did they, begod?

Nan So off we go. (*LSW To Bernard*) Take us away, Bernard. (*Loudly to Ellen and Ted*) We've been unmasked I'm afraid. We've got to go to the police station.

Nan bundles Ted and Ellen to the exit. Alec pushes Matt and Tim after them.

Matt (*LSW*) I've no objection to adlibbing, my dears. But I must be told what the play is.

Alec (*To Matt and Tim*) You've got to take them away.

Tim God, if I knew the crowd was out there –

Matt When did we decide on this script?

Ellen (*To Ted as they go off*) Keep away from me. Don't dare touch me.

Ted (*To Ellen as they go off*) I wouldn't touch you if they paid me a thousand quid.

Alec and Nan have by now bundled everyone off, except Bernard. Ted and Ellen are heard shouting and arguing in the wings. Bernard and Alec are left onstage.

Alec Well?

Bernard Well?

Alec All over.

Bernard Looks like it, old boy.

Ellen and Ted arguing in the distance.

Alec The end of the line.

Bernard Indeed.

Alec For them.

Bernard For us all, old man. For us all.

Alec Goodbye, Inspector.

Bernard (*LSW*) I never got to say my speech about the drinks. (*Going off*) Come to that, I hardly got to say any bloody thing.

Alec is alone: Ted and Ellen still arguing in the distance.

Alec (*To audience*) Well, I'm glad that's over. The guilty getting their comeuppance. And – and the whole affair turning out happily for me. (*He waits: then shouts towards where they have gone off*) I said the whole affair – which has now come to an end – turns out happily for me. (*Very deliberately*) And so – there's no more to be said.

The arguing in the wings gets louder: other voices besides Ted and Ellen can be heard. Alec waits, then: I know. I'll nip out to the kitchen to see if it's going to rain.

He runs off. The arguing grows louder and builds to a climax as the curtain come down. There is a pause. Then, very slowly, the curtain rises. Everyone, except Tim, is sitting around the stage. They are very still. No one says anything for a while.

Alec (*After a long pause*) God.
Nan Don't.
Alec I mean.
Nan Please.
Matt I thought you were doing Gaslight.
Alec If only –
Nan Forget it.
Alec And then –
Nan Please, Alec.
Alec You're right.
Nan Please.

Pause

Matt What happened to Gaslight?

Pause. Tim comes in.

Tim Excuse me. (*No one takes any notice of him*) There's – there's someone here. He wants to know if he can come in.
Nan Who?

Enter Billy, breezily.

Billy Me!

Billy wears a small hat on the side of his head. He has a loud tie pin in his tie: he wears a brown mohair overcoat slung over his shoulders. He should have an air of great dash and elan, yet there is something slightly shabby about him. Ellen and Nan jump up. The others remain seated. Tim moves to side, watching, very impressed by Billy.

Nan Billy!
Ellen It's Billy!
Billy (*Going to Nan, kissing her*) Darling! How are we, Nano?
Nan Oh, all right, Billy, all right.
Billy You look ten years younger.
Nan It's lovely to see you, Billy.
Billy (*Looking at Ellen*) And – now just let me think – it's – it's – it's Eileen, isn't it?
Nan Ellen, Billy.
Billy Ellen, of course, Ellen. (*He releases Nan, goes to Ellen*) How are you, Ellen? (*He kisses her*)
Ellen Fine, Billy, Fine.

Billy (*Still with an arm around Ellen*) I didn't know you had such super looking women in the company these days, Matt. I'd never have left if I'd known you were going to have women like this around the place.

Nan You haven't changed, Billy.

Billy Never change, Nan, never change. That's my motto. (*He goes to Matt*) And how's old Matt these days, eh? Still the big man we always look up to. We were talking about you, Matt, the other night in the television club. It seems we're always talking about you in the television club. Everyone of course either knew you or had worked with you and had yarns and funny anecdotes about you in abundance. But when it came down to it the only one who'd really done his stint with you was yours truly, Billy himself here. They all want to be in on the act these days, they all want to have started with you, Matt, or to have brushed shoulders with you somewhere along the way. But Billy's the man who can give them the low-down about you, Matt, started with you, stayed with you, learned everything I know from you, learned the basics of this rough oul' trade. And it's stood me in good stead, I can tell you.

Nan You've done very well, Billy.

Billy Mustn't boast, Nan, mustn't boast. I put it all down to what I learned from the good man himself here. (*Indicates Matt*) Oh, there's plenty of jumped-up Johnnies and fly-by-nights around these days who've done shag all and whose experience, genuine, real McCoy stage experience, is null and bloody void. But to listen to them you'd think they'd been born into the business and worked everywhere from the Moscow Arts to to the West End. But when I mention Matt here and what we used to do in the old days, Shakespeare, Shaw, Oscar Wilde, the lot, remember, Matt? the smile switches to the other side of their gobs, I can tell you. No, they can see where I got it all from, where the real groundwork was done.

Nan You were always loyal to the company, Billy.

Billy Why wouldn't I be? Where would I be without it? It's all down to you, Nan. Down to yourself and Matt.

Nan It's good of you to say so, isn't it, Matt?

Billy No more than is due. No more than is due.

Nan By the way, Billy, did you get my letter?

Billy I did, Nan.

Nan And – and what do you think?

Billy I think it was a lovely letter, Nan. You said some nice things in it.

Nan No, about – Well, about the play – ?

Ellen Nan wanted you to come back and do a play with us, Billy.

Billy I'd love to, Ellen, love to.

Ellen You would?

Billy I would.

Nan (*Excited turning to the others*) There! What did I say?

Ellen Nan said you'd come back, Billy.

Billy Every chance I get I never miss. It was the funniest thing tonight. I was down in Wexford opening a new foodstore. They like to have a bit of a celebrity at these things. It does no harm for the old image, if you understand my meaning, and, for a layer of icing on the cake, there's a nice little fee to go with it. Not, you know, to be sneezed at, in these dangerous days, when you don't know how the wind will blow tomorrow. Well, there I was driving back to Dublin, when I spotted the signpost to here. Matt and Nan's there to the end of the week, says I to meself, so off I turned and here I am.

Nan (*Clapping her hands*) I knew you'd come, Billy.

Billy I slipped in at the back and saw the last half hour of the show.

Nan (*Stunned*) The last half hour of tonight's show?

Billy Aye.

Ellen Oh, God, no, not tonight's show.

Billy Tell us, will you, when did you start doing gag?

Matt Doing what?

Billy Doing a gag show?

Matt We have never done such a thing.

Billy You could have knocked me down with a feather when I realized what it was. We never did gag shows in the old days.

Matt (*Rising*) Was that what was taking place tonight?

Billy And when I saw yourself coming on, Matt, in the middle of a gag show, well –

Matt (*To Nan*) Who gave permission for this? I want to know whose idea it was.

Nan I'm not sure whose idea it was. But I gave permission.

Matt *You* did?

Nan Yes. We couldn't do Ideal Husband without Leonard.

Billy (*Smiling*) Dear old Leonard done a bunk again, has he?

Nan (*To Matt*) We didn't want to repeat Gaslight. There was hardly anyone in for it the other night. And we had no new show ready. So it seemed a reasonable idea for getting on something quickly.

Matt I have never tolerated that kind of thing in my company. Never.

Billy I know you haven't, Matt. I know you haven't. That's why I was so staggered when I saw it. Absolutely staggered.

Ellen You picked a bad night, Billy.

Nan You see, business has been atrocious, Billy. That's why we need you to come back and do something with us. Your name would bring them in.

Billy That's nice of you to say so, Nan.

Ellen Oh, it would, Billy. They're always talking of you everywhere we go.

Nan You can decide what play you'd like to do. We could run it for a week at some good date. Or do odd nights in various dates. Whatever fits in with your plans best, Billy.

Billy I'd love to, Nan. God's truth, I really would. Love to. But the problem is how to fit it in. You see, I've got this and next week free, but then I start rehearsals for the new series and that carries on for about fifteen weeks.

Ellen Well, after that, perhaps.

Billy After that I'm doing this new play in Dublin. The Gaiety's already booked. Haven't you read about it? It's by John McMahon. You know, he wrote that novel everyone was reading a year or two back – all that small town sex.

Ellen Oh, The Road to Ballymore. I read it.

Billy That's the one, Ellen, that's the one. Well, he wrote this play with me in mind. We've great hopes for it. One or two of the London managements seem interested as well. And when all that's over, there's another series lined up for the box. So you see it's a question of time. Time: the great enemy. If I could fit in something with the company anywhere along the line you know I would. Nothing I'd love to do better. You know that, Nan. But, as you can see for yourself, it's out of the question.

Nan Out of the question?

Billy Totally. There's just no time, Nan. That's the problem. No time at all. (*Looking at his watch*) And talking of time, will you look at the hour that's in it. I've a drive back to Dublin before me yet. I must be taking a sod out of it. Pity it's so late. We could all have adjourned to a cosy snug for a natter about old times.

Nan (*Sitting: Dejected*) Yes.

Billy (*Turning to Bernard*) Eh, Bernard, what's this I hear about you doing commercials?

Bernard Well, actually, old boy –

Billy (*Ignoring him*) No better man for the job. Great type. I was going to give you a ring a few months back. They were casting a smashing part for an episode in the series – a retired colonial type – just up your street. But they flew over a character from London. Typical. And says I there'd be none better than our Bernard for the job.

Bernard That was rather – ah –

Billy (*Looking at his watch*) Must buzz. (*Going over to Ellen*) 'Bye, love. Give us a tinkle when you get back to Dublin. Never know – I might be able to put in a good word for you in the right ear. Know what I mean?

Ellen Thanks, Billy. But – I don't know your number.

Billy Jot it down. It's 36421. My flat number. (*Winking*) My personal number – just for special friends. Understand?

Ellen (*Who has got a pencil and piece of paper from her handbag*) What was it again?

Billy 36421.

Ellen (*Writing*) 36421.

Billy That's the ticket. (*Putting his arm around her*) Be sure to give me a call. (*He gives her a kiss, then turns to Nan*) Cheers, Nan. Sorry about the play.

Nan Oh, that's –

Billy Maybe sometime in the future. When things let up a bit, Eh, Matt? You and I must get together and do something really good again. Really cracking. Something that will set this bloody island alight. That's a promise, what?

He moves to the exit. Tim steps out in front of him. Holding out a pencil and piece of paper.

Tim Would you mind, Mr Brien? For the missus. She'd be over the moon. Never fails to watch you every Tuesday night.

Billy (*Taking pencil and paper*) Pleasure. (*Writes*) There we are! (*Hands pencil and paper back*)

Tim (*Reading*) With all good wishes. Billy Brien. Oh, God, thanks, sir. The missus'll be in her seventh heaven when she sees this.

Billy Glad to oblige. (*Turning to the others*) Always glad to oblige.

Tim retires to back looking at the autograph. He squats on a chair.

God bless, everyone. Keep up the good work. Remember, as far as Billy's concerned, the Monahans are still the best.

Billy goes out. They look after him. No one speaks for a long time. Everyone is still. Then Nan stands up.

Nan Well, that's it. I'll write out the notice tonight. It'll be on the board tomorrow morning. The tour will end Saturday of next week.

Matt The tour will *not* end.

Nan Yes, it will, Matt. I refuse to keep it going out of our savings. We've lost about six hundred pounds in the last year. If we go on at this rate in a short while we'll have no savings left.

Matt I will not allow the tour to end. If we can't afford to go on as we are, then we can do concert tours – recitals – excerpts from Shakespeare and all the plays we've done over the years.

Nan You still have to pay actors, Matt. We can't afford it.

Matt Then I'll do it on my own. I'll give solo recitals. Convents, schools, colleges, one night stands. I won't need scenery. I won't need even a chair. I'll stand on the bare stage with a spotlight on me if they've got one and with any sort of light if they haven't, and I'll do it all by myself. I have waves of energy surging through me, through every bone in my body and I am not dissipating it by sitting in a garden deckchair sleeping in the sun.

Nan You don't have to, Matt. There's plenty of work going on television. Radio. All sorts of things. Perhaps the odd bit of filming. Look at Billy.

Matt I have no wish to look at Billy. I have never had any wish to look at Billy. He's welcome to his television. It's where he belongs.

I belong here. On this stage. In these surroundings. In front of real people – no matter how few, exercising my craft, my trade, which God has put me on this earth to do.

Nan (*Turning to the others*) I'm sorry everyone. We've tried to keep going. As you can see Matt is prepared to lose every penny we have. I'm not. So the notice will be up in the morning.

Ellen It's a bit sudden, Nan. Coming just like that. I know you warned us. Still – it's a bit sudden.

Nan I'm sorry. I really am.

Ellen (*Gathering up her things*) One has given good service over a few years. It wouldn't have come amiss to have known about it a little longer. (*Rising*) I must give Billy a ring when I get to Dublin – he might put me on to something. (*Searching her bag*) Where did I put his number? I wrote it down. Jesus, don't say I've lost it. I know I – Here it is. Thank God. (*Reading as she goes out*) 36421.

When she has gone Ted looks at Alec. Pause.

Ted She'll get what she's looking for there.

Alec Aye: Billy won't fail her.

Ted Good luck to him.

Alec Good luck to the both of them.

Short pause.

Ted D'you – d'you feel like a jar?

Alec I wouldn't say no.

Ted We'll tap Donovan's back window. He'll slip us in.

They both rise.

Alec That's the best notion you've come up with this two years.

They go. Long pause.

Nan You'd better get to bed, Bernard. You've had a long day.

Bernard (*Rising*) Yes.

Nan Pity it wasn't last night Billy called. You could have had a free lift with him to Dublin for your commercial this morning.

Bernard (*Moving to the exit*) Darling, I'd rather cadge a lift off Hitler. I'd feel I was in better company. (*He stops, turns to Matt*) By the way, Matt, about this recital tour of yours. If you – if you'd like me to join you in it, old man, I'd be more than willing. We could do some of our two-handed scenes. And I could help out with the odd soliloquy.

Nan It would be no use, Bernard. There would be no money in it. Matt wouldn't be able to pay you. I doubt if he'd even pay his own expenses. You'd just be throwing away what you'd saved.

Bernard Oh, well, it was simply an idea, my darling. Anything to keep me from going back to bloody Poole.

Bernard goes out. Nan looks at Matt for a moment.

Nan Let's go. (*Pause*) It's late. You should be in bed. You need the rest.

Matt I've been resting all evening. I've been resting while you've been dragging the company down to its lowest point ever.

Nan Yes, well, it's all over now. There will be no more gag shows. No more appalling business. No more anything. Goodbye, the Monahan Players.

Matt A real pro never says goodbye.

Nan I must be getting past it then. I can't wait to give it a final wave of my hand. I can't wait to be surrounded by my own four walls and my patch of garden at the back. And the sight of Howth across the bay. That's the big thing in my life now: our own home. Our own four walls. After a lifetime in digs, rooms, flats, bedsitters, we now have our own place. Our own place. D'you know, Matt, I don't think you realize what those three words mean to me. I could kiss the walls, the floors, every time I go back to them. I do sometimes. Well, maybe, not kiss them, but I run my hands along them, fondle them: the wood, the plaster, the stones. No landlords, no landladies. Other people's places. You can never call your soul your own in other people's places. They have it over you as long as you're on their territory. No matter how nice they are, no matter how good a tenant you are. But with your own walls around you, your own roof above, your floorboards below, you can turn your back on the lot of them.

Matt I think you want the tour to end.

Nan I thought I didn't – maybe I was wrong. (*She gets up, moves to the door, stops*) Billy said a funny thing tonight.

Matt That'll be the day – when that character says something funny.

Nan We must get together and do something really good again, he said. Something that will set this island alight. Does that not remind you of something?

Matt No.

Nan It was what that critic said about you in that lovely play you toured England in for nearly a year. Matthew Monahan, he wrote, lights up the stage every time he walks on to it.

Matt I don't remember.

Nan I remember. (*Searches in her bag*) Never forgot it. There! Look! (*She takes a newspaper cutting from her bag, hands it to him*)

Matt (*Reading it*) Matthew Monahan lights up the stage every time he walks on to it. (*To Nan*) You mean – all these years – in your bag – ?

Nan Yellowing and tattered now, I fear, but yes. I've always treasured it.

Matt (*Quietly, slowly, almost to himself*) Lit – up – the – stage. It was always what I felt a good actor should do: light up the stage. And it was – secretly – what I believed I did when I was at my best, but no one had ever said so. Only that critic. That one man. And I've never stopped blessing him ever since. (*Absentmindedly, unnoticed by Nan, he puts the cutting on a table*)

Nan (*Smiling*) And you didn't remember! Ah, sure, don't the good notices go with an actor to his grave.

Tim (*Coming in*) Oh, God, I'm sorry, sir – sorry, ma'am. I just came in to turn off the lights.

Nan It's all right. We're just leaving.

Tim I didn't know ye were rehearsing.

Nan No – no –

Matt (*Still in his own thoughts*) Rehearsing. Yes. Ideas for a small recital tour, d'you see.

Tim Oh, I see, sir.

Matt Odd scenes. A soliloquy or two. Very simple, you understand.

Tim Understood, sir.

Nan (*Slumping on to a chair*) God, I'm exhausted. I need sleep.

Matt I was thinking of speeches from some of my best parts.

Tim (*Squatting on a chair on the other side away from Nan*) They'd be the exact ones to do, sir.

Matt (*Moving a few steps down stage, hardly aware of the others*) All the world's a stage. And all the men and women merely players. Yes. A good beginning. Very important – a good beginning.

Tim A truer word you never spoke. When I start the sweeping in the morning, them's the words I say to myself.

Matt They have their entrances and their exits – no – no – exits and entrances – yes – exits and entrances – haven't played it for such a long time, you see.

Tim I *do* see, sir.

Nan Always did well in the school and convent matinees. As You Like It.

Matt Splendid production in Dublin – the Gaiety.

Tim Oh, I'm sure, sir.

Matt Nineteen – nineteen -

Nan Packed them out in the Gaiety.

Matt One of my best parts. London – and then of course the Australian tour – and – and –

Tim I had a cousin somewhere in Australia.

Matt Yes – and one man in his time – one man –

Tim Another cousin in Manchester.

Nan We played Manchester.

Tim Or Ramsgate – one of them cities.

Matt Iago in Sydney. Marvellous audiences.

Nan And the Cork Opera House.

Matt Cork always a good date. And Belfast Opera House – two week season – just come back, d'you see – back to Ireland – Nan's idea –

Nan It was.

Tim Ah, there's always th'oul pull to come back, ma'am. Sure, there's no place like home. I always say: There's nowhere to beat Ireland. Not that I've ever been out of it.

Matt We settled to a pattern: Dublin seasons – touring –

Nan That's where the money was: touring.

Tim Oh, there's money around if you know where to put your hand on it.

Matt At first – at first the infant – mewling and puking in the nurse's arms –

Nan Marvellous business wherever we went. And Sunday nights, there wasn't even standing room.

Tim Ah, don't be talking, sure, two flies fighting one another here on a Sunday night and the crowds pushing in'd be fierce.

Nan Small village. Big town. Queues lining up for seats at the door.

Tim And if Mr Sweeney was taking the stage, they'd be coming in their thousands.

Matt – and then the whining schoolboy –

Nan And then – of late –

Matt – the whining schoolboy –

Nan Everyone blames television.

Tim Don't talk to me about that thing! Staring at that oul' box!

Matt – with his satchel – with his satchel – and his shining morning face –

Nan Don't know. Not sure. But these last few years –

Tim Oh, things have been tough these last few years down these parts.

Nan Even the good dates.

Matt – the whining schoolboy – with his satchel – his satchel and his – with his satchel – with his –

Nan Yes: even our good dates.

Tim Oh, indeed, ma'am.

Nan Even those.

Matt has stopped speaking. His hand is out in front of him. Slowly, his hand drops to his side. Nan looks at him, she gets up, goes to him, takes his arm.

Nan Come on. Time to go.

They walk to the exit door and stop. Nan looks around the stage and looks out front.

God, we've played some places in our time, Matt. But this – this –

They look out front. Pause. Then slowly Nan leads Matt off. Pause. Tim rises, makes his way across the stage. He sees the newspaper cutting on the table, picks it up, looks at it, then runs to the exit, calls after them, waving the cutting in the air.

Tim Sir! You've left your – eh, ma'am – you've left the –

He realizes they have left the building. He looks at the cutting and reads very slowly:

Matthew Monahan – lit up the stage – every time – he walked on to it.

He tosses the cutting aside, it falls to the floor. He reaches inside his pocket, takes out the piece of paper with Billy's autograph, reads:

With all good wishes – Billy Brien.

Going off, his voice filled with delight:

Wait till the missus sees this!

He goes out. After a moment, areas of light on the stage go out, one by one, until there is only one small area of light left in the centre of the stage. A pause. Then it too goes out and there is darkness.

ROADS TO INCHICORE

The play had a rehearsed reading in the main auditorium of the Soho Theatre, London on May 1st 2003 with the following cast:

Liam Lalor Roddy
Paddy Niall Buggy
Dicko Damian O'Hare
Angie Aislinn Mangan
Peg Nicola Redmond
Denny Patrick O'Kane
Sheil Gabrielle Reidy

The play was directed by the Soho Theatre Associate Director Jonathan Lloyd.

ROADS TO INCHICORE

Characters

Liam
Paddy
Angie
Peg
Denny
Sheil

The play takes place on the green at the edge of an Irish midlands town. The time is the present. It is summer.

Liam, Paddy, Denny, Peg and Sheil are in their mid forties. Angie and Dicko are in their mid twenties.

ACT ONE

Scene one
Lights come up. Paddy, Liam and Dicko are playing pitch and toss.

Liam The strike.

Paddy It's not the strike.

Dicko No, not the strike, Liam.

Paddy The strike was two years ago, for Christ sake.

Liam They warned us. If the strike went ahead, the factory'd close.

Paddy That was bluff. Bluff and shite talk.

Liam How was it bluff, Paddy? The factory's closing, isn't it?

Paddy Aye, it's closing *now*. But they didn't close at the time of the strike, did they?

Dicko Market forces.

Paddy Market, my arse!

Liam They said it in the letter. Market forces were compelling them to close their operation in Ireland.

Paddy The letter! D'you know what I did with that same fucking letter? (*His hand to his bottom*) I used it in the jacks!

Dicko Good man, Paddy. I knew you'd find a use for it.

Liam And now there are rough days ahead for us all. No work in the town. A bad time for yourself and Angie, Dicko. If you were thinking of –

Dicko Ah, now is not the hour for Angie and myself to be thinking of marriage, Liam.

Paddy Aye, it's about time we caught a sight of that Celtic fucking Tiger in this locality.

Liam I was a barman in Dublin. As soon as I heard that this Dutch firm was starting up the shoe factory outside the town I was on the next bus home.

Dicko And married Peg?

Liam Oh, no, Dicko, Peg and me weren't married for a few years after I came back.

Paddy And don't forget to add, Liammy, old son, that you had to wait till Peg had finished with Denny Lenehan before you could share the marriage bed with her.

Liam Ah – Denny and Peg – there was nothing to that. Only teenage stuff.

Paddy He put an engagement ring on her finger.

Liam It was never a real engagement, Paddy.

Paddy 'Twas a real fucking ring. I saw it with my own eyes.

Dicko Is that so now?

Paddy That is so. Them two – Denny, Peg – wouldn't be seen apart. Kissing, fondling each other. You'd see them – then come summer, the swimming out there by the river. The rest of us'd be diving, jumping, splashing, swimming – them two – they'd be lapped thirty times round one another on the grass –

Dicko What – Peg and Liam?

Paddy No! Peg and Denny. Peg wouldn't even glance at poor oul' Liam here in them days.

Liam Innocent goings on – that's all.

Paddy Innocent? Father Naylor didn't view it as innocent.

Dicko I never knew Father Naylor.

Liam Father Naylor died before you were born, Dicko. A heart attack at the start of High Mass.

Paddy At the finish of Benediction.

Liam I thought it was High Mass, Paddy. Didn't he go down at the start of the Creed?

Paddy He went down as he sang Tantum Ergo.

Dicko Tantum Ergo is Benediction.

Paddy Father Naylor was informed of the carrying-on up the swimming place.

Dicko So is O Salutaris.

Paddy Father Naylor wasn't having that behaviour before the youth of the town. Sure, 'twas fucking well corrupting the rest of us. He spoke of it from the altar.

Dicko (*A little smile*) He didn't speak, did he, Paddy, about yourself and Sheil, by any chance?

Paddy (*His mood darkening*) Myself and Sheil? What have you to say about myself and Sheil?

Dicko I was only thinking as yourself and Sheil – (*Observing Paddy's change of mood*) Ah: nothing. Nothing – I was saying nothing.

Paddy You were saying nothing nothing, were you?

Liam It's best to be saying nothing. People's lives are nobody else's business.

Paddy (*Threatening*) Are you telling me, Liammy, oul' son, that what I'm saying about Denny Lenehan and your missus, Peg, is none of my business?

Liam Ah, God, no, Paddy. That's not what I'm saying at all.

Paddy I'm glad that is not what you're saying at all. Because, Mr Liammy, no one tells this boy in this locality what is his business and what is not his business.

Liam (*Quietly*) No, Paddy.

Paddy (*Looking at the coins – probably ten p. pieces – on the ground beside the stone*) No. (*Slight pause*) Now, who's nearest?

Liam I think I got there, Paddy.

Paddy Aye, I believe so. You always get there in the finish, Liammy, is not that correct?

Dicko You got there, Liam, all right once Denny Lenehan was off the map. And talking of the same Lenehans, 'twas sad about the mother.

Liam The Lord have mercy on her soul.

Paddy The Lord have mercy on *whose* soul?

Dicko Denny Lenehan's mother.

Liam Died out at Notre Dame.

Paddy No one informed me of this news.

Dicko Oh, that didn't stop her dying, Paddy. You not being informed of it.

Paddy But there was no talk of Mrs Lenehan dying. When a person dies, there's talk of them dying before they die.

Dicko Well, sometimes, Paddy, they die without any talk of them dying. No: poor Mrs Lenehan died last night.

Liam In the early hours of this morning. So she'll be taken to the church tomorrow night. Before or after midnight: that's what counts.

Dicko Is that so, Liam? The midnight, is it, makes the difference?

Liam The midnight's the thing to keep in mind. Die before midnight tonight and you go to the church tomorrow night.

Dicko But die after midnight?

Liam And you go to the church the night after tomorrow.

Dicko So – it's this way, is it – that if you want to be taken to the church on, say, Friday night, you have to die on the Thursday night?

Liam Any time before midnight on the Thursday and you're safe as houses for the Friday night.

Dicko But after midnight on the Thursday?

Liam Oh, if you leave it till after midnight on the Thursday, you've missed the boat for the Friday. You'd have to wait till Saturday night in a case like that to be taken to the church.

Dicko So it comes down to it in the end, does it, that the day of your funeral is fixed all according to whether you die before or after midnight on a certain day?

Liam You have it now. It's no use dying after midnight on Wednesday night if you're anxious for your funeral to be on the Friday.

Dicko In that case, your funeral would be on the Saturday.

Liam Exactly so.

Paddy It's a bloody complicated business, this dying.

Liam It's as easy as drinking a pint once you've got the hang of it, Paddy.

Paddy (*After a pause*) I wonder if Denny will be home?

Dicko It's most likely he'll be home for his mother's funeral.

Paddy I wonder, now, will he? Sure, his sister Molly hasn't a bloody clue where he is.

Dicko The dad often talks about Denny. The dad and Denny were pals.

Paddy We were *all* pals. Your dad. Liam, there. Denny. Myself. But of course Denny always had other things on his mind You know, Dicko. Involving the missus there. (*Indicates Liam*)

Liam Is it your throw, Dicko?

Paddy 'Twas Peg, Peg, night, day with Denny at that time. Right, Liammy?

Liam Ah – that's all in the past.

Paddy Begod, we hope it is. It'd be a bad case if it was still in the present with Peg now wife and mother down in that fine house of yours, Liam.

Dicko If Denny turns up for his mother's funeral –

Paddy Oh, if Denny turns up for his mother's funeral, it mightn't be so much all in the past, you're spot on there, Dicko. Denny being in the town again might bring the past flowing back in Peg's mind.

Liam Look: I think we should get a few more games in.

Paddy I suppose Peg never reminisces, does she, about the old days with Denny?

Liam (*Quietly*) No.

Paddy Ah, that's understandable. A wife wouldn't want to recall the days when there was a fellow she'd been messing about with before she joined her groom at the altar.

Liam Are we having a game?

Dicko Maybe it's a pity we haven't Denny still up at Reikharts. He worked there before he left the town. Maybe he'd do something for us.

Paddy Do something?

Dicko Aye. Maybe he's the sort of man'd speak up for us and stop the factory shutting. I mean if them bastards, Maguire and the strike committee'd done their job –

Paddy Don't mention in my presence Maguire and that committee. That committee's job was to give us workers the will to stay out.

Liam If the workers haven't the will to stay out, it's asking a bit of the committee to give it to them.

Paddy That's where you don't understand labour relations, Liammy. It's the workers' leaders duty to stiffen the morale of the workers.

Dicko Why can't the workers stiffen their own morale?

Paddy (*Very loud*) 'Cause that's not the workers' fucking job! That's the leaders' job. Leaders! That blow-in Maguire from up the black north. Antrim or some god forsaken hole. A bloody Orangeman!

Liam Ah, fair's fair, Paddy. He's a good Catholic.

Paddy Catholic or Orange he hails from beyond the border. We should have nothing to do with any of that crowd. It seems to me it's a good thing the border is there to keep that bloody lot o' lunatics at a distance.

Dicko Look at the flag-waving eejit that was in the town a year or two back from Derry or Armagh or some bloody backwater up there, the shop assistant. You couldn't get in a word before he was off on his fucking jet plane about discrimination and partition and second class citizens and a united bloody Ireland.

Paddy If a bloody Ireland united –

Dicko Ireland shagging united!

Paddy If it means we have the likes of that maniac in this town, then, for my money, you can keep your united fucking Ireland.

Dicko The Queen of England's bloody welcome to him.

Paddy And then we go and put one of them clowns in charge of our union.

Dicko If Denny Lenehan –

Paddy Denny Lenehan! Just because Denny Lenehan packed in the job and went to England, doesn't mean he's anything special.

Dicko No, Paddy, – 'twas just – I thought – he might be – might be – a man to lead us –

Liam No – no – but Dicko might be on to something there, Paddy. Denny had – didn't he, now? – he had something about him – we have to admit that – you know –

Paddy (*Annoyed*) What something about him? What?

Liam Well – remember the way Denny'd be forever yapping on about a thing he'd read – a book – or – or – you know – maybe – poetry in the paper –

Paddy Poetry in the paper! That was all to put himself above the rest of us. We were the clod-hopping bog eejits, but he, the great Denny Lenehan, was the guy for poetry in the fucking paper. He's no different from you or me or Dicko there.

Angie (*Coming in over the bank L*) Hi.

Dicko Hi.

Liam Oh, hello, Angie.

Angie Hello, Liam. (*Turning to Paddy*) And how's the man, Paddy?

Paddy Paddy's all right, thank you very much for your concern in asking.

Angie And what do the men think of the news that we'll all be on the dole in two weeks' time?

Liam Bad, Angie. Very bad.

Angie The whole town's scuppered. Shops, pubs, trades people.

Dicko We were discussing it just now. We were saying the union men let us down.

Angie What could the union men do?

Paddy They could fight, couldn't they?

Angie Why couldn't *you* fight, Paddy? Why couldn't Liam there and Dicko, why couldn't they fight?

Paddy And yourself. You're up there too. Why don't you put up a fight?

Angie 'Cause I haven't the guts. Just like the rest of you. We leave it all to Maguire and the union and little thanks they get for their trouble.

Paddy You'd like to give them thanks, wouldn't you? Especially Maguire, with his wavy hair and his big smile. This lady of yours, Dicko, has a great regard for Maguire's wavy hair and big smile, were you aware of that?

Liam Now, now, Paddy!

Dicko (*Sneering*) Maguire!

Liam Aye, but what could we do, Angie?

Angie We had the chance two years ago when Van Druthen asked us to sit down with him and –

Paddy – and discuss cutting our wages!

Angie Yes, a temporary cut. To get the company through a bad time.

Paddy It was the union's job to sort that out.

Angie Hotheads like you wouldn't let them.

Dicko Eh, careful there, careful, that's Paddy you're talking to.

Angie That's Paddy you're talking to! Jesus, there you have the whole life of this friggin' territory.

Paddy (*Laughing*) So: I'm a hothead, am I?

Angie You *were* at the meetings. We never for once brought our brains to work on any of it. It was oul' shouts and slogans and stupid songs sung across in Hickey's pub.

Dicko We were part of the true union movement in them days. Workers together! 'Twas a stirring time.

Angie So bloody stirring it brought about the shutting of the factory.

Liam I don't think, you know, we ever should have gone along with the strike.

Angie You should have said that, Liam, at the time. But you didn't. 'Cause you knew loud mouth here – (*She indicates Paddy*)

Dicko Eh, here, now, Paddy's no loud mouth. You're not a loud mouth, are you, Paddy?

Paddy (*Very loud*) We were right to strike!

Dicko We made a stand. Isn't that right, Paddy? Stood our ground.

Angie Stood on our bloody heads. And let our brains into our boots.

Paddy Are you saying, miss – is it this what you're saying – that it's *our* fault the factory is closing?

Angie Yes: that *is* what I am saying.

Paddy I'm not standing here and listening to this talk. That's what's termed scab talk. Yellow belly talk from a little bitch like that!

Angie You have no objection, have you, Dicko, to hear me called a little bitch?

Paddy If you have, Dicko, express your objections now. To that madam that's supposed to be your girl called a little bitch.

Dicko (*To Angie*) Don't cross swords with Paddy. Paddy's my mate.

We're all together in this. Workers. You have to stand by your mates.

Angie Standing by our mates has got us into this. If we'd had the gumption two years ago not to stand by our mates the factory would not be pulling down the blinds.

Paddy I'm over to Hickeys for a drink. I have taken that decision. I have no wish to be in the company of Miss slut-face talking scab talk.

Angie You were always quick with the nice phrase, Paddy. You heard what he called me, Dicko?

Dicko Ah, now, Paddy –

Paddy Yes, Dicko? Have you something to say to me?

Dicko (*Quietly*) No, Paddy.

Paddy Good! You'll join myself and Liammy across in Hickeys. And after that we'll wander down and pay our respects to Molly Moran. Molly Lenehan, as was. About her mother.

Angie Denny Lenehan's home from England for the funeral. Flew over early this morning.

Paddy Denny Lenehan home! There's news now! Would you not say so, Liammy?

Liam (*Quietly*) Aye, Paddy.

Paddy We might bump into him across in Hickeys. He'll be anxious, no doubt, to enquire of you after Peg. So over we'll go. Come, Dicko.

Angie Dicko: I want to talk to you.

Dicko I'm crossing to the pub with Paddy and Liam. I'll see you down your place later on.

Angie If you go, Dicko, you've gone for good.

Paddy And what does that dramatic pronouncement signify?

Angie It's none of your business what it signifies.

Dicko (*To Angie*) Will you watch your language there with Paddy! (*Moving*) I'll see you later.

Angie There's no later, Dicko. You stay now and talk to me. Or you go for good.

Liam Come on, Paddy, *we'll* go. Leave them together.

Paddy (*To Dicko*) Jesus, have you no guts, man? To let the bitch dictate to you like that.

Angie No bitch ever dictated to you, Paddy?

Paddy By Christ, they did not!

Angie That's why, no doubt, you've got such a wonderful relationship between yourself and Sheil.

Paddy (*Threatening*) What did you say?

Dicko (*In quickly*) She said nothing, Paddy. (*To Angie in a low angry voice*) Why don't you shut up!

Paddy (*Approaching Angie*) Don't think because you're a woman I wouldn't – By Jesus, I'll thrash th' arse off you, if ever again –

Angie I know you would, Paddy. You have it in you.

Dicko Go on, lads. I'll join you in a minute.

Paddy You most certainly will not join me if you choose to stay with that little whore. Your great and perfect love! Messing about with Maguire in th' Arcadia th' other Saturday. Don't you see the bloody fool she's making of you?

Liam O.K., now, Paddy, come on, we'll go. See you, Dicko. See you, Angie.

Paddy Aye, Liammy. Leave the little shits. One as bad as th' other. We'll clear the air with a drink on our own. (*Going*) Over we go.

Liam and Paddy walk over the bank L and leave.

Dicko What th' hell did you say that for? He nearly had me a few minutes ago just mentioning her name. You know how touchy he is about Sheil and himself.

Angie And so he should be. The way he's messed up that poor woman's life is a disgrace. Keeping her dangling like that years, getting all the goodies out of the relationship, but taking care not to marry her.

Dicko He's not the marrying type, Paddy.

Angie No: he's the exploiting type. Meals down at Sheil's house – and I expect the rest that goes with it. Does he ever take her to the pictures up the Ritz or to a dance?

Dicko Ah, they're beyond their dancing days.

Angie They're beyond all days now.

Dicko Well, that's their business.

Angie You're right. I should be minding my own business. But that's the way of it in this town: your business is everyone's business. That's why it's a good thing Reikharts is shutting.

Dicko What the hell are you on about? It's the worst disaster that's ever hit the town.

Angie I'm not talking about the town. I'm talking about me. It's a disaster for the town the factory shutting, it'd be a disaster for me if it wasn't. 'Cause it'd mean I'd be staying on here.

Dicko 'Course you're staying on here. This is a good place to live. Gerry Boylan who travelled every corner of Europe couldn't wait to get back to settle here.

Angie Jesus, Europe must be in a bad way if that's the case.

Dicko (*Looking towards the pub*) I'd better – you know –

Angie You're happy to drink with that guy even though he slaked you off and degraded me with his low language.

Dicko Yah, he didn't. You know Paddy.

Angie Too bloody well. Come down the river with me. We can talk.

Dicko Talk – talk! What d'you want to talk about?

Angie What? I want to – (*Stops*) What I'm trying to say – (*She stops speaking. Pause. She walks a few paces, sits on a stump of tree*) What *am* I trying to say? Jesus, I don't know. (*Pause*) You and me, Dicko. Reikharts closing. It's made me think. At least, it's had that good side to it. While the high wages rolled in I just jogged along, not thinking. Now, Dicko, I have to think. Me and you. How long has it been now – five, six years? Nothing's ever been said out in the open between us. You took me for granted. I took *you* for granted. You never asked me for a more permanent stake in your life. I don't know if it's even in your mind. My fear is – this is my fear: that we might turn into Sheil and Paddy. Or even if we *do* get married, that we might turn into Peg and Liam. (*Pause*) I don't know how Peg will feel when she sees Denny home for his mother's funeral. She was mad about him, they say. But he just jacked it in at Reikharts and took off for England. (*Pause*) So: what's before us?

Dicko The factory's shutting, that's what's before us.

Angie Even if they were not shutting, that question would still be in the air between us. But as they *are* shutting, what are you going to do?

Dicko I'll draw the dole, like the rest of them. You will too.

Angie And you and me?

Dicko Ah, what's wrong with the way we're going? Why d'you want to turn everything upside down? We're O.K. But you'll stop hanging round Maguire. I won't have that. That bloody Orangeman, Catholic though he is. You danced with him half the night in the Arcadia.

Angie I did. In fact, I danced with him the *whole* night.

Dicko And you can sit there and tell me that?

Angie Yes. Because I want to be honest with you. I don't want a Paddy and Sheil situation.

Dicko Ah, forget bloody Paddy, will you!

Angie I wish I could. But as long as you're in this town, Paddy won't let you forget him. He drips into every corner of life. I only mentioned him, 'cause I don't want to do as he does: having the best of Sheil, but, at the same time, giving nothing in return. No, I'm being honest with you. That's why I'm telling you Maguire drove me home from the Arcadia.

Dicko You came home in the car with the girls you went with.

Angie No, you assumed I did.

Dicko And what took place?

Angie Where?

Dicko In Maguire's car. After the dance.

Angie I'm being honest, Dicko, but I'm not being *that* honest.

Dicko I've a right to know.

Angie No, you have no right. A while ago I would have said you had. But since I've got to thinking – the factory shutting brought that on – I've decided you have no rights, as far as I'm concerned.

Dicko We're –

Angie What? We're what? I mean – what? Are we going to get married?

Dicko It's not the time to get married, is it, with the two of us embarking on the dole?

Angie And we exist on the dole, do we?

Dicko We're lucky to have it. 'Twould be a bleak outlook without it.

Angie It seems to me to be bloody bleak *with* it.

Dicko Look: I'll come up to you after I've had a drink across.

Angie No, Dicko, you won't come up.

Dicko I will. I'll only be an hour.

Angie You can be the rest of your life, for all I care. You'll never come up to me again. I'll never come anywhere with *you* again. I'd like to say it's ended between us, but I can't, because it's never even begun between us. Begun properly. But whatever there was – and there was the odd good laugh, I will say that – whatever there was is now finished. There wasn't much there, but I'm putting a stop to it. I have a great need to do that. Not to drift with the tide any more.

Dicko Ah, you're feeling down, that's all it is. Sure, the whole town's in the same boat. The dole won't be so bad, you'll see. We'll be O.K. (*Pause*) The – the lads – beyond – you know – (*She is turned away from him*) – we'll be all right – you'll see – we'll be – aye –

He slinks off over the bank L. Long pause. Angie rises, walks slowly to the pitch and toss stone. She sees a coin on the ground. She picks it up, looks at it, turns it over. While she is looking at the coin, Denny comes in R. He stands looking at her. Angie tosses the coin to the ground. She turns to leave, sees Denny.

Denny Hello.

Angie (*Surprised there is anyone there*) Hello.

Denny No one here.

Angie Ah – no.

Denny I thought I might find some of the lads here. Summer evening. Pitch and toss. Always used to be here.

Angie They're across in Hickeys.

Denny Ah: Hickeys! The centre of wit and conviviality and sparkling talk. Doctor Johnson's coffee house recreated in darkest Leinster.

Angie (*Smiling*) I wouldn't go that far.

Denny You are – ?

Angie Angie. Angie Dowling.

Denny Which Dowling would that be?

Angie Owen Dowling's daughter.

Denny How is Owen?

Angie You know him?

Denny I was at school with him.

Angie You must be – ? You're Denny Lenehan?

Denny (*Mock bow*) A votre service! As Mrs Hickey would say – pulling a pint.

Angie (*Going to him, her hand extended*) I'm pleased to meet you.

Denny (*Shaking hands with her*) And I'm very pleased to meet you, Angie.

Angie I've often heard about you.

Denny (*Smiling*) I'm big here, am I?

Angie (*Laughing*) Very!

Denny I've achieved something in life after all! (*He moves away*)

Angie (*After a pause*) I'm sorry about your mother.

Denny Thank you, Angie.

Angie She was a nice woman. Many's the ten p. bag of liquorice I bought off her. I remember the sign over the shop. Bon-Bon. That was such an exciting sign to me as a kid. Bon-Bon!

Denny High class confectionary. Licensed to sell tobacco.

Angie (*After a pause*) What's it like, Denny – London?

Denny It depends what you're looking for?

Angie What were *you* looking for?

Denny I've only known you five minutes and you ask me a personal question like that.

Angie Did you miss it when you went, Denny? The town?

Denny No.

Angie Not anything – or anyone?

Denny Let's stick to anything. I missed something. I could never quite define what it was exactly. The country round here – a bit. The people – the ways of doing things – the way of talking – no. In the end, I used to say I missed Ireland. I was never sure what I meant by that. But the town – even coming back to it now – only for a few days – I feel I'll never get away again. I hear keys turning in locks, bolts being slammed shut.

Angie I've wondered if I'd miss it.

Denny Are you thinking of leaving?

Angie Playing with the idea. Reikharts is closing. You heard that? (*He nods*) Of course you worked up there yourself.

Denny What will you do?

Angie What most of them'll do: draw the dole. I don't want that. If Dicko'd – (She stops) You know Dicko? Dick McCann. Matt McCann's son.

Denny I knew Matt.

Angie If he'd shake himself and make a move, I might – you know – Dublin, maybe. Or somewhere in England. Or further afield: the States. Maybe Australia.

Denny The long chant of the young people of Ireland: England, The States, Australia. Where to go? Most of us come face to face with it. Maybe, it's different now: the Celtic Tiger, the EEC, all that. But there's an itch in the Irish genes spurring us on to get out, take a look at a wider world. And when we do make a move, the tug is always there, the never ending pull, the spark to keep on the move or go back to where you came from. It's a ritual once begun goes on forever.

Angie If Dicko –

Denny He's your – is he? Your man, your boyfriend, fiancé?

Angie To tell you the truth, Denny, I don't know what the hell he is. We go to dances, the pictures. We fumble the odd kiss in his oul' fella's car. That, Denny, is high romance as it happens in this town at the beginning of the twenty first century.

Denny (*Laughing*) I recognize that picture. I sat as a model for it more than once.

Angie Was it like that between you and – ? (*Pause*) Sorry, sorry, Denny, I've no right to – sorry.

Denny (*After a slight pause*) I'd rather hear about you and McCann's son.

Angie There's not much to hear. He'll never shove the boat out from this shore.

Denny And you want him to? Why do you want to go, anyway?

Angie Why did *you* want to go?

Denny We were talking about *you*.

Angie (*Moving around*) I'm not a very fascinating topic to talk about. What do I want? I just feel I don't want what's here. I left school as quick as I could, got the job in Reikharts – good money. I wish now I'd stayed at the books a bit longer. I hear people talk – on the radio, on television, I read things in the paper or in magazines and – Jesus – listen to me!

Denny Go on.

Angie And – you know – I only half latch on to them. It's like something you want to get hold of – a balloon in a breeze – and it's floating away all the time – you grab to catch it – and it's – it's –

Denny Out of your reach?

Angie Out of arm's length – that's it. And I feel it'll always be out of my reach if I stay here.

Denny Going away, Angie, going to England, America, whatever, very often doesn't make all that difference. Things can still be beyond your reach.

Angie I know. So what's the solution, Denny?

Denny What's the problem? That's what you've got to find out before asking what the solution is.

Angie I think there's a problem. If you can't see what it is, no one can.

Voices off L. Paddy, Liam and Dicko come in over the bank. They stop talking and stand on the bank. Pause.

Paddy (*Staring at Denny*) Jaysus! Look at the man. Will you look who it is. The fellow himself.

Denny Hello, Paddy.

Paddy Am I seeing things?

Denny Hello, Liam.

Liam Hello, Denny.

Denny How's Peg?

Blackout

Scene Two

Lights up on Paddy and Liam playing pitch and toss. They play for a while before speaking.

Liam Went off well.

Paddy What went off well?

Liam Mrs Lenehan's funeral.

Paddy Why d'you say it went off well. You're not talking about the All Ireland Final. A funeral can't go off well. The person's dead, isn't she? That's not going off well. It's going off dead.

Liam I was just talking.

Paddy You were talking as if it was a bloody race meeting. There's people whining and moaning every corner you look.

Liam I meant there were no hitches.

Paddy The woman was dead, wasn't she? You don't call that a hitch?

Liam But she didn't die at the funeral, did she?

Paddy Be Jaysus, it was lucky she didn't. If you waited till she died at the funeral, there'd be no bloody funeral in the first place.

Liam No, I mean the sadness of her dying. That was *before* the funeral.

Paddy Of course it was before the funeral. It's a prerequisite of having a funeral to begin with for the sadness of the person dying to have occurred at some time beforehand.

Liam (*Subdued*) I only said it went off well.

Paddy Went off well! What does it mean – went off? Went off where? If things go off, they go off to some place. I went off to Dublin.

Liam Did you, Paddy – when?

Paddy No, I bloody didn't! I'm only saying – as an example of words meaning what they say. The meeting went off well means nothing, unless those present at the meeting started walking or running –

Liam Or travelling in cars.

Paddy They'd hardly be travelling in cars if they were at a meeting, would they? What I'm saying is: only if those at the meeting moved –

Liam Unless they had mobile phones. They could all be travelling in cars holding their meeting through mobile phones.

Paddy Forget mobile bloody phones! I'm trying to get it into your thick head unless there's movement to another place, you can't say the meeting went off well.

Liam (*Pause. They play*) Like: getting on. You say: How is he getting on?

Paddy How is *who* getting on?

Liam No one. But it doesn't mean what it says. Getting on means getting up on something. Like getting on a horse or getting on a bike. But when you ask someone: How are you getting on? – you're not talking about getting on a horse –

Paddy Or getting on a bike. You're asking: How are you doing?

Liam Ah: there's another one! How are you doing? That really means: How are you doing something? Like: making a table or fixing a lamp. But when you ask a person: How are you doing? – you're not asking: How are you doing making a table or How are you doing fixing a lamp?

Paddy Put your mind on the game and forget about fixing a bloody lamp. (*Pause. They play*)

Liam A pity, wasn't it, we couldn't go to the cemetery? Had to fit in the church in our dinner break. The mother of an old friend!

Paddy That Maguire should have insisted we had time off. But he's not interested in us now that he's fixed himself a job up North.

Liam Has he, by God?

Paddy He's a no-good. Look the way he treats Dicko. Messing about with that tart, Angie.

Liam Ah! D'you think, Paddy – should I say this, I wonder – d'you think – how would I put it – there's a thing going between herself and Maguire? I mean: Angie belongs to Dicko.

Paddy Angie belongs to anything that can be loosely designated a paid up member of the male species. Maguire and – and ogling Denny Lenehan here th' other night.

Liam Tell me, Paddy – how d'you think Denny was looking?

Paddy Old. He looked old.

Liam (*Pleased to hear this*) Aye: I thought so too.

Paddy The years – as we say – have not sat well upon him. (*Pause*) What did Peg think?

Liam (*Quietly*) She didn't say. She didn't say what she thought.

Dicko comes in briskly along the path R.

Dicko Went off well enough, ha, lads? The funeral.

Paddy Jesus: he's at it now!

Dicko I thought it did. Didn't you, Liam?

Paddy (*Loudly*) Shut up! Shut up! (*Slight pause*) Went off well!

Dicko Oh, you didn't think it did, ha, Paddy?

Liam I've just thought, Paddy. The funeral went off well is O.K. to say, 'cause it *did* go off: it went off to the cemetery.

Dicko That's where a funeral goes, Liam: to the cemetery.

Liam No, Dicko, d'you see, Paddy and myself were talking about the way we say things.

Dicko There's only one way to say where a funeral goes: to the cemetery. The cemetery is a funeral's natural finishing point.

Paddy It's the natural finishing point for the whole bloody lot of us. Funerals! Cemeteries! For Jesus sake, pack it in! I'm sick of funerals and dying and the dead.

Liam You have to think of it, Paddy, if it happens to you.

Paddy But it hasn't happened to me. I'm alive, amn't I?

Dicko Mrs Lenehan isn't alive. It's happened to her. She's dead.

Paddy She'd better be. Else they've made a right cock-up shoving her in the ground today.

Liam (*After a pause*) Dicko: what did *you* think of Denny?

Dicko I thought he looked great.

Liam (*Disappointed by this reply*) Did you? I thought he looked old.

Dicko Ah, no, I'd say he was a few years younger than the two of you.

Paddy (*Angry*) He's bloody not younger than me!

Dicko Isn't he, by God? He doesn't look it then.

Paddy (*Angry*) What d'you mean he doesn't look it? If anything, I've weathered the storm the best of the two of us.

Liam You have, Paddy. You're a finer looking man. The years have sat well upon you.

Dicko Oh, the years have sat well upon you, Paddy, no denying it. But they've sat well upon Denny too.

Paddy (*Shouting*) No, they bloody haven't, they bloody well have not! What are you building up that bastard for? Just because he's been to London, he's taken you in. Like he's taken your girl in. Or that bitch you were fool enough to call a girl.

Dicko What does that mean, Paddy?

Liam Ah, Paddy means nothing, Dicko. (*Angie appears on the bank: they don't see her*)

Paddy Look at the way she was preening herself for him – the Londoner – when we came upon them returning from Hickeys the other night. Christ, it makes me laugh the way ye all fall for it.

Dicko I don't think I fall for it, Paddy.

Paddy Yes, you do. Just as you let that bitch Angie go hopping the slip jig with Maguire.

Angie (*Calmly*) Sheil would never go hopping the slip jig with any man these days, would she, Paddy? You've seen to that.

They turn: see her.

Liam Oh – Angie!

Angie (*To Paddy*) There's no danger of Sheil casting her eyes at any man or any man casting his eyes on her, because, Paddy, you've turned her into an old woman. And I hear once she was a lovely girl. Sheila: she was known in the town, they say. Now she's Sheil. Your Sheil.

Dicko (*A loud whisper*) Shut your face!

Paddy Who's put you up to saying this?

Angie I'm saying it myself, Paddy. This town connived, or, at best, stayed silent, while you converted her into old woman Sheil from young girl Sheila.

Dicko (*Loud whisper*) Watch your lips, girl! Pay no attention, Paddy. Turn your back on her. Come across. We'll have a drink. (*Moving*) The turned back. That's what they can't stand.

Paddy Aye. (*Turning his back on Angie*) You're right. We'll go across. (*Paddy and Dicko move left. They walk up the bank. At the top Paddy stops Dicko with a hand on his arm*) But you'll promise me one thing.

Dicko What's that, Paddy?

Paddy You'll promise me, as long as you're a friend of mine, you'll never have anything to do with that low woman. 'Cause if you do, you're no friend of Paddy's.

Dicko I'm a friend of Paddy's. No debate on that point. A friend of Paddy's.

Paddy Good. We'll go then. (*They go off. Pause*)

Liam Well – Angie –

Angie Well – Liam. (*Slight pause*) Any – any sight of Denny this evening?

Liam No, Angie. Hasn't been up this way. (*Slight pause*) I'll go across. (*He goes left, stops, turns to her*) All that. Dicko – ah – he doesn't mean the half of it. You've got to let things pass over your head, Angie.

Angie And if you can't let them pass over your head, Liam?

Liam Well, that's a bad case then. But you have to try. It's the only way to get through.

He goes. Angie sits on the bank, then lies back, her arms under her head. After a while Peg comes in cautiously along the path at the right. She looks to see if anyone is there. She doesn't see Angie she walks around, stops at the pitch-and-toss stone, looks down at it, picks it up, juggles it in her hands. Angie, sensing someone is there, sits up.

Angie Peg!

Peg (*Turning*) Angie!

Angie Are you looking for Liam? He's gone across to Hickeys with the lads.

Peg (*Letting the stone fall to the ground*) No – no. Just – you know – a walk – such a grand evening –

Angie Oh – sure. (*She gets up, comes down to Peg. She is smiling*) It's a rare sight to see you down this way, Peg.

Peg Yeh. I haven't much interest in the pitch-and-toss.

Angie The pitch and toss! And Paddy – tribal chief of his pitch and toss kingdom.

Peg Oh, Paddy – God bless him! (*Angie laughs. Pause*) And how's Dicko?

Angie How's Liam? (*They both laugh*)

Peg Enough said – sorry I asked! (*Peg stretches out her arms, looks up at the sky*) Oh, God, Angie!

Angie What, Peg?

Peg (*Moving a few paces, her arms still outstretched*) I don't know. I don't know.

Angie No. (*Pause*) And – Reikharts shutting –

Peg Ah, they can shut it, keep it open, I don't give a balls, Angie.

Angie It'll be a loss to the town.

Peg It will. I'm only thinking of myself, the selfish bitch I am.

Angie There'll be a big clear out. There's talk of Dublin, England, the States. Larry Egan is going to Canada. It's all you hear. People packing their suitcases.

Peg Leaving the rest of us behind. Being left behind, Angie. It's the worst feeling in the world. (*Pause*) You and Dicko – ?

Angie No, Peg. No way. Not now. End of line.

Peg (*A slight pause*) Is he thinking of going away?

Angie Ah –

Peg Might be the best thing, Angie. If he wants to make a new life somewhere. Oh, it seems hard at the time, to tear yourself away – the pull of family, the habit of familiar places. But, in the long run, they're deceptive things. Good things, aye, but unless put in their proper place, they are things that, with time, can turn into prison bars. I had the chance to go. I was begged to go. Fear held me back. I let fear win. And now I'm hemmed in by prison bars. You'd have different names for them: Liam, my sons, my marriage, this town, my house. I call them iron bars of a jail. (*Pause*) If Dicko wants you to go with him, go, Angie. Don't hold back for the things that one day will put you behind bars.

Angie (*Quietly*) Dicko doesn't want to go. His great ambition now is for a life on the dole in this town.

Peg And you?

Angie I'll not draw the dole, Peg. Some of us can have a good life here. Some of us can't. Why that is, I'm not really sure. I think now I'm one of the ones that can't. That's a pity, maybe. For me more than for the town. The town will get on without me. Whether I can get on without this town, I'll have to find out. Denny seems to have managed it.

Peg Just because he comes back with a big smile on his face doesn't mean he's got this town out of his guts.

Angie No. (*Pause. Angie moves away, does not look at Peg*) Peg.

Peg Mmm?

Angie I hope you won't mind me saying this. And – you know – it was a long time ago with you and Denny. And you have Liam now and your boys.

Peg Yes?

Angie (*After a pause*) I – I like Denny.

Peg Well, he's a likeable fellow.

Angie No: not just "like". I think it's more than that.

Peg (*Sharply: turning on her*) How could it be more than that? You've only seen him at a distance at the funeral today. You can't get to like a fellow more than that at a distance.

Angie I had a long talk with him the other night.

Peg (*Surprised*) Where?

Angie Down here. We talked while the lads were across in Hickeys. And – I like him.

Peg He can give you twenty years any day. Old enough to be your father.

Angie Well – nearly. (*Slight pause*) I think – I might like to go back with him. To England.

Peg (*Annoyed*) Oh, for God's sake, will you cop yourself on, Angie. You know nothing about Denny. Did you know he was married in England?

Angie No, I didn't know that.

Peg Well, he is.

Angie That didn't stop you coming down here hoping to bump into him.

Peg What are you talking about?

Angie Didn't you?

Peg (*After a pause: quietly*) Did I? (*Pause*) You're right: I did.

Angie Surely – all that's in the past, isn't it – you weren't thinking of – ?

Peg I don't know what I was thinking of, Angie. I was just hoping to see him again. Hoping to talk to him. I saw him today at the funeral and – I haven't talked to him in over twenty years.

Angie (*Looking towards the path right*) Well – you can talk to him now. He's coming along the path.

Peg (*Rushing to the bank left*) Oh, God, I can't, Angie. No: you stay, I'll go. Please!

Angie (*Indicating left*) I'll hang about beyond. If Liam and the lads come out of the pub, I'll tip you the wink. (*Pushing Peg towards centre*) Go on.

Peg (*Nervous*) Angie –

Denny comes in right. Angie walks up to him.

Angie There's an old friend of yours here, Denny. (*He sees Peg*) I'll be seeing you.

Angie crosses to the bank and goes out left. Denny comes to centre: Peg turns to him.

Denny Peg.
Peg Denny.
Denny How are you?
Peg Fine.
Denny Good.
Peg Yourself?
Denny Fine.
Peg (*After a slight pause*) I'm – I'm sorry about your mother.
Denny Thanks.
Peg (*After a pause*) So.
Denny So.
Peg Yeh. So. Here we are.
Denny Here we are.
Peg A long time.

Denny Very. (*He walks around*) The pitch and toss green.

Peg Still here.

Denny What changes?

Peg Little, Denny, very little. (*Pause*) And London?

Denny Oh, plenty changes in London.

Peg I heard that.

Denny Crowded. Noisy. Not unlike this place on a wet wintry Sunday.

Peg Wet wintry Sundays make up a lot of hours here.

Denny Those hours were my teenage years.

Peg (*Smiling: pause*) I heard – I heard you married.

Denny You heard a lot of things.

Peg You didn't bring her home? To view our borough?

Denny No.

Peg How could you deny her such an experience?

Denny Cruel: I admit.

Peg I'd have thought she'd have come over for her mother-in-law's funeral.

Denny She has another mother-in-law these days.

Peg (*Obviously pleased*) Oh? So – so you're single again?

Denny I suppose that's the proper job description.

Pause. They both begin speaking at the same time.

Denny It's – / **Peg** I'd – (*They stop: laugh*)

Denny After you.

Peg No: you first.

Denny Oh, I was just going to comment on the great weather.

Peg I was going to say – sorry.

Denny What for?

Peg You know what for.

Denny What's being sorry mean?

Peg Sorry means sorry: that's all there is to it. No, it's not all there is to it. Sorry means sorry I didn't do what you asked me to do: go with you.

Denny Probably the best decision you ever took.

Peg For you, maybe. (*Pause*) You went. I stayed. I married Liam.

Denny He's a good man.

Peg The best. Kind: decent. He'd give me the world if he had it in his gift. He's that kind of man. That's the kind of man he is.

(Laughter of men off left)

Denny (*Walking left*) The boys over in Hickeys.

Peg Oh, Hickeys! You never liked it over there.

Denny No? I seem to recall evenings of scintillating banter and jocularity under Mrs Hickey's benevolent gaze.

Peg Mrs Hickey's benevolent gaze wasn't to your liking.

Denny You remember that?

Peg I remember everything. I've spent twenty years remembering. (*Pause*) And I remember the poetry you used to say to me.

Denny You do?

Peg "I will arise and go now and go to Innisfree – " We learned that at school with Miss Higgins. But you saying it to me down the river was the first time I took any notice of it. Saying poetry, writing poetry, 'twas all you could talk about one time.

Denny Was it?

Peg You know well it was. Your head was full of the stuff. (*Slight pause*) Is she – was she interested in poetry?

Denny Is Paddy interested in metaphysics?

Peg (*Smiling*) He might be! Except I don't know what the hell metaphysics is. (*Slight pause*) She was Irish, was she?

Denny As the Liffey.

Peg You don't have to tell me if you don't want to.

Denny Not much to tell. No: she didn't like poetry.

Peg What *did* she like?

Denny A good salary cheque coming in every month for me. A fairly large house, the latest car, smart clothes, smart friends, or those she kidded herself into thinking *were* her friends. And she adored pushing me up the slope of promotion in the job.

Peg What job was that?

Denny Sales assistant in a shoe shop.

Peg A shoe shop?

Denny A shop for the purpose of purveying footwear.

Peg (*Smiling*) And did she manage to get you up the slope?

Denny Very successfully. I got to manager.

Peg Manager! And it was all down to her, was it? Your – wife?

Denny I think it was, yes.

Peg She must have been pleased.

Denny Thrilled. Especially when an even bigger job showed its head above the horizon.

Peg What job was that?

Denny Area manager. Eleven branch shops under me across a wide stretch of the South of England.

Peg God, that sounds a great job to have.

Denny It was. Except I didn't have it. I turned it down.

Peg Turned – ? You didn't! Why?

Denny Oh – reasons. Mainly, I suppose because that wasn't what I'd come to England for.

Peg What *had* you gone to England for?

Denny Not that. In fact, it was why I left Reikharts. I didn't want any of that. I was good at the things I didn't want.

Peg If you stayed in Reikharts – you might have had something you *did* want.

Denny Mmm?

Peg Yeh – me. (*Suddenly changing, pretending to make light of it*) Still: no point dancing that dreary old waltz again!

(More laughter from the pub)

Denny The lads are in good form this evening.

Peg The lads. D'you know – those same lads would give their right arms to be offered jobs like that. None of them ever were. They couldn't even get to be charge hand up at Reikharts. Van Druthen liked you: he'd have given you something good up at the factory. But – no, you threw that chance away. (*Suddenly turns to him*) You threw a lot away – here – in England – that others have striven half a lifetime for.

Denny Others are welcome to it.

Peg (*In a rush*) Tell me, Denny. What is it you want? What is it you're after? You didn't want Reikharts. It seems the shoe firm offered you a good position in England: you didn't want that either. Most of us have to settle for what we can get. A lot of the lads here – the women too – are sick to the pit of their stomachs with the factory closing. And you go chucking over good jobs that they can't get within a mile of. You turn your back on everything and everyone and on any chance that comes your way. (*Emotional: loudly*) Who the hell d'you think you are?

Denny (*Quietly*) No one, Peg. I don't think I'm anyone.

Peg (*Controlling herself*) Sorry. Sorry. It's none of my business speaking to you like that. I'd better go. The pitch-and-toss boys will be out of Hickeys any minute. (*Slight pause*) I won't say it's been nice seeing you again. If I said that, it would get nowhere near what I mean. (*Pause*) When – when d'you go back?

Denny Tomorrow most likely. I've – ah – a little job to get back to.

Peg A – *little* job? Not running branch shops over half England?

Denny Nowhere near. A very humble post, I fear. Paddy and the boys would laugh the roof off Hickeys if they knew.

Peg I won't tell them.

Denny It little bothers me whether you tell them or not. For God knows when I'll be seeing them or this place again.

Peg That sounds final.

Denny My departure from this town is always meant to be final. But it never is. The mark of the place is always upon you, the trace of it always deep down in your guts wherever you go, whoever you're with. I've spent twenty years trying to get this town out of me. I think I've finally handed in the towel.

Peg That's why you never came back, was it, why you cut yourself off from everything and everyone? I'm sorry. I'm saying things I've no business to say. And today, the day of the funeral, they are things I'm sure you've said a thousand times to yourself. (*Slight pause*) So – anyway – before I go, I have to say it: it's terrific seeing you again.

Angie (*Appearing on the bank L*) Peg: there's movement at the pub door.

Peg Thanks, Angie. (*Angie stands on the bank, looking off and occasionally* *looking at Peg and Denny*) She said she'd tip me the wink if she saw sight of the boys.

Denny (*Indicating Angie*) She seems a nice kid.

Peg Angie? (*Turning to him, concerned*) You think so?

Denny Owen Dowling's girl, she tells me.

Peg (*Lowering her voice, making sure Angie can't hear*) Ah, she's all right. But she's a bit – you know – inclined, to be honest with you, inclined to be flighty.

Denny (*Smiling*) That's being young, Peg.

Peg (*Clearly worried about how Denny regards Angie*) Is it? Is being young spreading yourself around? She's supposed to be steady with a lad we call Dicko – you'd know his father – but she's no one man band, Miss Angie isn't.

Denny Yes, she told me about Dicko. She said she didn't know exactly what they had between them.

Peg I'm not surprised she doesn't know what they have between them! 'Cause – truth is – she's off with every second fellow giving her a sideways glance. (*Piling it on against Angie*) There's a lad up at Reikharts – the union man – she's been hopping off to dances with, unknown to Dicko. If I was a man – if I was – let me tell you – oh, yes – I'd steer well clear of Madam Angie.

Angie (*A loud whisper*) Peg!

Peg (*To Angie*) Aye. O.K. (*To Denny*) Maybe I'll see you before you go back.

Denny Maybe.

Peg No: not maybe. Promise me I will. If only to say goodbye properly. You never said goodbye to me properly.

Denny I'll say goodbye to you properly, Peg.

Peg Great. I can go now. Now – now that that's settled. (*She turns to Angie*) Thanks, love.

Peg goes out. Angie comes down to Denny

Angie You wanted that, didn't you? (*He looks puzzled*) To be rid of her.

Denny They're not coming from Hickeys?

Angie Ah, you can never tell whether they are or not. She can be a drag, Peg. So I thought I'd give you some space from her.

Denny (*Looking at his watch*) I'd better be getting back –

Angie Are you still married, Denny? (*He is surprised at the question*) Peg said you were married. I don't see your wife.

Denny (*Smiling*) But I see a young lady I barely know asking me the most intimate questions!

Angie (*Entering into the jokey spirit*) Ah, go on: you know me well by now! You and her split up, isn't that it?

Denny That's it, is it?

Angie I think it is. (*Pause*) Denny.

Denny Mmm?

Angie Can I walk down the town with you?

Denny What about – you know – Dicky – ?

Angie Dick–*o*!

Denny What if he sees you?

Angie Ah, if he sees, he sees! (*Puts her arm through his arm*) Come on! I'll walk you down the road. Give them something to get their mouths round with their Guinness beyond in Hickeys.

They go off down the path R. Paddy and Liam appear on the bank L. It is clear Paddy has been drinking. They see Denny and Angie going off arm in arm.

Paddy Ah – ha! Look a' that! Look a' that, Liam!

Liam (*Staring off R*) Jeez – look at that!

Paddy (*Calling off L*) Dicko! 'M'ere, Dicko! Where th' hell are you? (*Pointing to R*) Look – look a' that!

Dicko – a little unsteady from drink – appears on the bank L

Dicko (*Not yet seeing Denny and Angie*) Wha – ? Wha – Paddy?

Paddy (*Pointing to R*) Look a' that! Look a' that!

Liam (*Looking off R*) Dicko, look at that.

Dicko (*Looking R*) Jesus! Look a' that!

Blackout

ACT TWO

The green. Liam is pacing up and down. Dicko is sitting on a tree stump.

Liam Are you listening to me? Might be a chance. D'you know? If –

Dicko (*In his own thoughts*) Her arm – and his –

Liam We turned it down before. Maybe – maybe we should try it now.

Dicko Herself and the fucking Londoner.

Liam To keep the factory open. A cut in wages is better than no wages.

Dicko But – by Christ – I'll get him!

Liam Ah, oul' talk like that never got anyone anywhere. Now, this is my thought: if we formed a delegation, say, even at this late hour, approach Van Druthen –

Dicko Show that bloody Englishman.

Liam What Englishman?

Dicko That bastard Lenehan.

Liam Denny's no Englishman. He's as much a part of this town as you are or as I am.

Dicko I'd be doing you a favour too. You know – Peg and himself. You wouldn't want to see any of that again.

Liam Ah – Peg and Denny – all in the past.

Paddy (*Coming in from R*) Ha – ha! The boys!

Dicko (*Very down*) Paddy.

Paddy Oh – ho! Do I detect a note of dejection in that voice or what, me brave Dicko?

Dicko A bit cheesed off, Paddy, aye.

Paddy And I think I can surmise the cause. Yes, I do believe I can hazard a conjecture as to what the root of the discontent may be. I mean when our sophisticated friend from over the water comes back. Ah, yes! A king returned to his true domain. And all the women his for the taking!

Dicko Be the Jesus, Angie's no –

Paddy (*Seeing the effect on Dicko: piling it on more making a big gesture towards the ground*) And the men lie down beneath his feet!

Dicko By the fuck – I'll not –

Liam Ah, no use making a fuss.

Dicko Not make a – ? Fuss I will fuck well make!

Paddy (*Calmly*) Ah, I don't know if you would, Dicko. I don't think somehow you've got the balls for it.

Dicko (*Walking around vigorously*) By th' festerin' Christ, me – what – fuck balls – I've got – by Jesus, me – is it – ?

Paddy Ah, I don't know if we'd see that now.

Dicko You'll see it, Paddy. You'll Jaysus see it! See if you Jaysus well won't!

Liam But going after Denny: it won't keep us our jobs, will it?

Paddy Jobs! Ah, yes! That has just reminded me. I would go so far as to say it has recalled it to my brain. I overheard a funny little snippet walking down the main street two short minutes ago.

Liam (*Excited*) There's hope for us, is there? About the job, what?

Paddy The job: aye. Aye. But not *our* job. Someone else's. It was an overheard remark. Oh, yes, this certain personage gave up his job at Reikharts twenty years ago –

Liam Denny you're talking about – ha – ?

Paddy He was going to do great things in England. A roarin' Rolls Royce we expected him to return to us in.

Dicko A wooden shagging box he'll shag well end up in, the shagger, when I shagging –

Paddy Now, listen, the boys: are ye listening?

Dicko Listening, Paddy, by Jaysus, listening, I am, for when that fucker –

Paddy D'you know what the great man has for a job in England?

Liam I don't, then, Paddy.

Paddy I'll tell ye –

Dicko Tell – tell – what fuck big job – tell –

Paddy I'll tell. He has for a job – this will crease ye, lads – he has the exalted position of –

Dicko Of? Of?

Liam Of?

Paddy Of caretaker.

Dicko Caretaker?

Liam Caretaker of what?

Paddy Not Buckingham fucking Palace, that's for sure.

Liam Caretaker!

Paddy Sweeping up, sweeping out, cleaning the jacks, scrubbing, polishing, shining, locking up, stacking chairs –

Dicko Stacking tables.

Paddy Stacking every fucking thing.

Liam Taking care: it's what a caretaker does.

Paddy Taking care to keep the fact well and truly hid. The daily slog up Reikharts wasn't good enough for him. Though naturally it was good enough for us poor country yobbos. So he takes himself off to England and –

Dicko (*Laughing*) And lands up as a bloody caretaker! Stacking chairs for Her Majesty the Queen!

Paddy Stacking chairs for no one, queen, king or country! No: he went to England for great things. Big fellow of this.

Dicko Boss of that.

Paddy He'd come home flashing the notes.

Dicko With fast cars.

Paddy Gold watches dripping off him.

Dicko Silver watches wrapped round his arse.

Paddy Instead.

Dicko Instead.

Paddy Instead the lofty position he's attained is –

Dicko Caretaker! (*Laughing*) That's bloody good! Does Angie know?

Paddy Does Peg know?

Liam (*Pleased*) I'm sure she doesn't.

Dicko We'll tell them.

Paddy Tell them. (*As of giving an order*) Tell them. In fact – notify them!

Dicko Oh, we'll notify the entire town!

Paddy Acquaint the parish with the news.

Dicko We will! We will!

Paddy I would go so far as to say – promulgate it.

Dicko We'll prom – we'll pro – We'll do that, Paddy!

Paddy Promulgate and disseminate what he is.

Liam (*Still getting used to the news*) A caretaker! God!

Paddy The big impression, boys, that's the thing these returned wanderers try to put over on to the rest of us poor oenseochs.

Dicko The big story that they're doing well in England.

Paddy England or America. Australia or Canada.

Dicko New Zealand or Liverpool.

Paddy All parts of the known world. Australia, Canada, New Zealand, Liverpool. We fall for the –

Dicko At – at – that's right, Paddy – fall for the –

Paddy For what?

Dicko For – what you were going to say, Paddy.

Paddy How d'you know what I was going to say till I've fucking said it? That's the trouble with the whole bloody lot of you in this God forsaken hole. Never think for yerselves.

Liam I've been thinking for myself, Paddy. It's this: we should approach Van Druthen. Offer to take a cut. It might save the factory. Save our jobs.

Paddy What are we, Liammy? Are we slaves in the American South? You've heard of the American South?

Dicko *I've* heard of the American South. It's where the rhumba comes from.

Paddy Are we prisoners with chains on our legs down a Russian mine?

Dicko Be Jaysus, I never knew they wore chains on their legs down them Russian mines.

Paddy No. We're free Irishmen. Our forefathers fought for our freedom. And we're workers. It's an insult to the dignity of the working man to take a cut in his wages.

Denny (*Coming in R, clapping*) Great speech, Paddy.

Paddy (*Taken aback at seeing Denny*) Aye, great bloody speech. But it's a speech you'll never catch this boy making.

Liam Denny.

Denny Liam. (*Turns to Dicko*) Dicko, I believe.

Dicko (*Surly*) Dicko to my friends.

Denny I knew your dad.

Dicko Be Jaysus, that was a great start in life for my dad, wasn't it?

Denny Would you say so, Dicko?

Dicko Did you not hear me? I said I'm Dicko to my friends.

Paddy Dicko, d'you see, Denny, does not care for anyone to step on what he considers to be his private territory. He takes exception – I would go so far as to say he resents anyone who – encroaches.

Dicko Encroaches is the word, Paddy!

Paddy D'you see, he objects to infringers. Or to put it another way: to those who transgress.

Liam Well, Denny, all over now: the funeral.

Denny It is, Liam.

Paddy (*Annoyed that Liam has diffused the attack on Denny*) No, no, Dicko is a man who has strong views on these delicate matters.

Dicko There, Paddy, you've got the screwdriver right in the screw. And – and – (*Suddenly bursting out: turning to Denny*) Your fucking day is done!

Denny Sorry, Dicko?

Dicko (*Shouting*) Dick! It's twenty years on.

Denny Are you speaking to me, Dick?

Dicko No, I'm speaking to Elvis fucking Presley. You come here – you come – what you come here for?

Liam He came home for his mother's funeral.

Dicko The funeral's over. You can go back. To London – or wherever the fuck you belong. You're not wanted here. I know all about – I do – I know –

Denny Do you, Dick? Well, I'm bloody glad of that. Whatever it is you know.

Dicko You're no longer the young fellow here. Grey hair, middle aged. I'm the young fellow here now.

Paddy (*Laughing*) There's talking! There's talking, begod!

Denny (*To Dicko*) And a fine specimen of a young fellow you are, Dick, if I may say so.

Dicko You may *not* fucking say so! There's bare patches in your head. Noticed that?

Paddy (*Laughing*) There's words!

Denny Curiously enough, I *had* noticed that. My golden locks are not quite what they used to be.

Paddy (*Laughing*) Oh, begod!

Dicko (*Taken aback: not sure how to deal with Denny's attitude*) I – I – I – saw the – the photo of the minor footballers. My dad and yourself and Liam there on the team.

Denny (*To Liam*) What a fine body of men we were in that photo, Liam.

Dicko (*To Denny*) Your – your hair black in that photo. A full head of hair.

Denny Oh, very full! The Irish electorate voted it the best head of hair ever seen in the province of Leinster when the question was put to them in a referendum.

Dicko (*Again flustered*) Listen – listen – listen, will ya – hear this – your – your days as a minor are gone.

Denny Thank Christ, they are, Dick. I couldn't wait to be rid of them.

Dicko Peg is well married here to Liam.

Liam Oh, now, Dicko –

Dicko Angie could be your daughter. She's mine. Angie's mine! But you – you –

Denny Me, me, Dick?

Dicko You – half your life over –

Denny Only half? Thank you for reassuring me on that point. Some days it feels as if most of it's over.

Dicko You – you have no say in it – any of it – Angie and me – London shit!

Denny I'm afraid that particular substance changes very little wherever you go, Dick. London, Dublin, here. It's much the same all over. Even New York, they tell me, varies hardly at all in that respect. Whatever our differences with the wider world, in that regard we're very alike.

Dicko Paddy there, Liam there, they stayed.

Paddy Well said, begod. Stayed. We did.

Dicko My father stayed.

Denny You make it sound like a disease, Dick. All that staying.

Dicko If there's no one to stay, there's no life.

Paddy (*Laughing*) There's talking!

Dicko (*Encouraged by Paddy*) Turn your back on the town –

Denny I'd never turn my back on this town, Dick. You could never tell from which direction the knives were coming.

Dicko Turn your back – then come here and –

Liam He can come home to his mother's funeral, Dicko. He has that right. After all, he was born here.

Denny God, you're right, I was, Liam. I suppose it's an oversight they've neglected to put up the bloody plaque.

Dicko Born here. And he left. Did he have to? No, he didn't! Others had to – and *will* have to – especially now with Reikharts closing.

Liam It's none – you know – of our business, Dicko. We can't tell Denny what he should do.

Dicko I'll tell him what to do!

Denny Somehow I feel extraordinarily confident you will, Dick.

Dicko I fucking will. Keep away – she's my girl – we'll be married –

Liam Ah, fair's fair, Dicko. He's only –

Paddy (*Cutting in quickly on Liam*) Keep away – aye – Dicko – you were saying?

Dicko I was saying –

Liam It's Denny's life. Sure, if he wanted to travel –

Dicko Travel?

Denny That's right, Dick. Sort of moving about – you know – by train, plane, ship or car. Bicycle or moped. Point A to point B.

Paddy (*Laughing*) Oh, Denny's travelled! He's travelled.

Liam Travelled. Seen the world. Sure, isn't that a great thing?

Dicko Seen the world? He's seen fucking nothing. The world?

Paddy (*Laughing*) There's speechifying!

Denny Big place, the world, Dick.

Dicko Fuck the world!

Denny *All* the world? Oh, that's a tall order, Dick. However well loaded one is in that department.

Dicko (*Shouting at Denny*) Caretaker! Travel off to be king of the world! Caretaker!

Paddy (*Pretend innocence*) Caretaker? What is this – caretaker?

Denny (*Very casually*) It's a job I do in London, Paddy.

Paddy Caretaker? I do not believe this intelligence. You were a man with big prospects, Denny. Reikharts was too small for you.

Liam Ah, he wanted to see a bit of life, no crime in that, eh, Denny?

Dicko (*To Denny*) And what great life did you see, please tell us.

Paddy (*Laughing*) Caretaker? No – surely – there's a mistake, Denny?

Denny (*Quite unconcerned*) Oh, no mistake, Paddy. That's what I do. I'm a caretaker of a hall.

Dicko A – caretaker of a hall?

Paddy Caretaker – of a *hall*?

Denny Aye, halls seem to attract caretakers, for some strange reason. You know: like fish and chips.

Liam Rashers and eggs.

Denny Laurel and Hardy.

Liam Russians and – Jesus, what goes with the Russians, Denny?

Dicko Fuck all goes with the Russians. Not fucking caretakers, anyway.

Liam A caretaker can be a good job.

Paddy Well, aye, aye, I suppose, looked at in a certain light, attaining to the position of caretaker *could* be termed an achievement.

Dicko Does the town know of this great achievement?

Denny What a sad gap in their education if they don't, Dick.

Paddy No, I do not believe the town *does* know that, Dicko.

Liam Sure, it's none of our – what's happened to Denny in England – you know.

Dicko What's happened in England is that all he was able to get was a job as a caretaker.

Paddy A *hall* caretaker.

Dicko Hall caretaker – that's all.

Paddy Is that all, Denny?

Denny That's all, Paddy.

Dicko That's all he does. Hall caretaker. That's all.

Denny That's all. (*Then – in a sudden rush*) And one room. Single room. Camden Town. A window. A view of brickwork. Black trees, grimy gardens, no sky or little, very little sky. Where's the sky? I roar out some mornings, they've abolished the sky by Act of Parliament, I roar. And pigeon dirt, telephone wires, electric cables, phone masts. And screech of traffic: buses, cars, taxis, trucks and milk floats, horns, shouts, screams in the night, screams in the day as well –

Paddy (*Puzzled*) Wha – ?

Dicko (*Puzzled*) What's he fucking – ?

Denny An armchair, Dicko.

Dicko (*Loudly*) Dick!

Denny A massive armchair, Dick. Soft. Warm. Small room. Twelve by twelve. Or thereabouts. Yes: twelve square. Feet I'm talking about, Dick.

Liam Feet in length, Denny?

Denny In length, Liam.

Liam In length, say, like inches or yards?

Denny Like, say, yards or inches, Liam. A bed, a cooker, sink in corner, table, kitchen chair, where, you ask, does it all fit, with that huge armchair stuck right in it? It fits, Dick, it fits, Paddy.

Liam Jesus, I'm glad it fits, Denny.

Denny Like a glove, Liam, a soft woolly glove. Lace curtains as well, the sun, the Camden sun, yellow, petrol fumed, oily, streaming across the worn down carpet. A hundred and fifty quid a week, plus electric bills and Council Tax, after work, late at night, sitting in that immense armchair, losing myself in it –

Dicko (*Puzzled*) For Jesus –

Denny Lying back, reading, sitting, all tension gone, muscles, nerves relaxed. Graham Greene, Dick.

Liam One of your neighbours, Denny, is that it?

Denny A good neighbour. And Joseph Conrad, Paddy.

Paddy Who? Who the fucking hell – ?

Denny Hemingway too, Liam.

Liam Ah – wait now, wait now – is this it? Your room in London, Denny, is that what it is? Have we got it right? You sort of sit in it and kind of – you know – read?

Denny Thomas Hardy at the moment, Liam.

Paddy You kicked the bejaysus out of a guy called Hardy, didn't you, Dicko, full back for Mountmellick, in the semi final a year or two back?

Denny Yeats and Joyce as well. Mustn't forget our own. Our own native land, Dick, what?

Dicko Don't you fucking talk to me about our native land, you bloody alien.

Denny And Charlie Dickens bringing up the rear. Feet up. Soft warm armchair.

Liam It's – it's what you like to do, Denny, right? I think I have you now.

Dicko (*To Paddy*) Is this guy having us fucking on?

Paddy (*Pointing to himself*) No one is having this guy fucking on!

Denny Walking the dark Camden streets. Books under th' arm. Night classes, Dick.

Liam They've night classes here in the Tec. Carpentry. All sorts. Cookery.

Denny English Literature, Liam.

Liam Flower arranging, they say, next winter.

Denny A mate took me along. Put me on to something.

Paddy What were you put on to?

Denny A thing.

Paddy (*Frustrated: shouting*) What fucking thing? What?

Denny A thing I was after, but didn't know I was.

Liam I'm with you now, Denny. In London you found it – ha?

Denny In the dingy dark Victorian heavy winter rain dripping North London Institute, Liam.

Paddy (*Shouting*) What did you find? What?

Denny A thing I didn't know I was going to find, Paddy.

Paddy (*Shouting louder*) What fucking thing you didn't know you were going to find?

Liam Sure, I see, I see, Denny. 'Twasn't till you went to London – ah, I see it now.

Paddy (*Shouting to Liam*) What d'you fucking see?

Liam I think – correct me if I'm wrong, Denny – 'twas something you discovered in London. Would I be there or thereabouts in that regard? A sort of – this is the way it's emerging to me – a kind of an interest. Have I hit it, Denny?

Paddy An interest? Nothing shagging marvellous in that. We got an interest. Th' oul' pitch and toss here.

Liam Aye, but Denny's interest – now here I think I'm on to it, eh, Denny? It's that – the – the books – the reading – d'you see, if I understand him correct – it took off – in London – and he likes –

Paddy Likes? What? What?

Liam Likes – sitting – have I it in the frame now, Denny? And reading – his room – you know – in London.

Paddy (*Confused*) Reading! For Jaysus sake!

Dicko (*To Denny*) Are you making mugs of us?

Denny Could I mix cement without water, Dick?

Paddy Sitting! Reading! We *all* shagging sit – read.

Dicko Don't shagging try that game.

Paddy Not here, mate.

Dicko Not bloody here.

> *Long pause. Denny has turned away. He has picked up the pitch-and-toss stone and is throwing it from one hand to the other. Pause.*

Liam But a book in the hand: sure, wasn't that always you, Denny? The books and the poetry. Aye, from when you were in the short trousers.

Paddy I mean – for Christ sake.

Dicko Taking the frigging Mick. The – the caretaker!

Paddy Well, you can understand him sermonizing about reading and books to draw the blinds down in front of us poor simple eejits, hiding the fact that –

Dicko – all he's done is get to be a caretaker.

Paddy A *hall* caretaker. Do not forget that!

Dicko Oh, a *hall* caretaker! I've taken note of that detail, Paddy.

> *Paddy and Dicko laugh. Their laughter dies.*

Liam (*Quietly: after a pause*) I read a book about the American Civil War. The whole lot of them went up in smoke in a wooden ranch house in the finish. Did you ever read that book, Denny?

Denny (*Quietly*) No, Liam, I never read a book about the American Civil War.

Dicko Why d'you have to go to America for a civil war? Didn't we have our own civil war here? Bejaysus, you'd have to travel far to find a better civil war than our civil war.

> *Denny throws down the stone. Angie and Peg come in along the path R.*

Angie (*Pointing at Denny*) There he is! The word was you'd gone back, Denny.

Denny Tomorrow, Angie. I came down to say so long to the lads.

Dicko Begod, then, you could have saved your shoe leather.

Liam Oh, now, Dicko. I'd like to wish Denny the best. An old school pal. Things from far back linger still.

Peg We were all the same time at school: Liam, Denny, Paddy, me.

Liam I'd like to shake his hand before he leaves us.

Paddy (*Laughing*) We know why you'd like to shake his hand, Liammy, and see him leave. Eh, Peg?

Peg Are you talking, Paddy?

Paddy I'm talking, Peg. Liammy too knows I'm talking. Right, Liammy?

Liam Ah, well, now –

Peg You've a lovely face, God bless you, Paddy, when no sound comes out of that shape you call a mouth.

Liam Now, Peg. Now, Paddy.

Paddy (*Very angry*) Ah, get away to hell. I could have had you if I wanted, when I wanted, but I turned my back on you.

Silence. No one speaks for a moment, then Dicko giggles.

Dicko Is that so, Paddy? (*Giggling*) Jay! Oh, Jay!

Paddy (*A little laugh*) That is so indeed.

Peg, smiling, walks very determinedly up to Paddy. She brings her face very close to his.

Peg If that is so, Paddy, if that was *ever* so, then I'm a dead woman. For if that was ever true, I'm dead and I was a dead woman all my life.

A laugh from Angie and Denny. Paddy, angry, makes as if to push her away.

Dicko (*Intervening*) Ah – ha! Remember, Paddy, the turned back. They hate that, remember?

Paddy (*Turning away*) Aagh!

Angie So you're off, Denny?

Denny I am, Angie.

Peg (*Coming away from where Paddy was*) Everyone's off, Angie tells me she's off too.

Liam You're off, are you, Angie?

Angie Yes, Liam.

Dicko, who is up with Paddy, suddenly turns to them.

Dicko Who's off?

Liam Peg says, Dicko, that Angie –

Dicko Off? (*Coming down to Angie*) Where, off?

Angie I am, Dicko. I came to find you to let you know. But I don't want to tell you with the town listening. Could we go somewhere quiet?

Dicko Quiet? For why?

Peg Because she wants to speak to you privately, Dicko.

Dicko Oh, I get it. You don't want to tell me with *him* listening.

Angie Him? Who?

Dicko The fellow you're off with.

Angie He's not listening.

Dicko Not listening? He's not deaf, is he?

Angie I bloody hope not. And, anyway, that's not the point. I wanted to tell you when we're by ourselves: just the two of us. I owe you that.

Dicko Out with it. What you have to say, say it. Before everybody. Let the bastard be seen by all for what he is. (*Confronting Denny*) And let them know that he's not getting out of this town without taking me on first.

Liam Ah, now, Dicko – we don't want any trouble.

Dicko I'll show the returned emigrant he can't pick and choose any woman he cares to take back to London with him.

Angie What woman is he trying to take back to London with him, Dicko? I'd be curious to know.

Dicko (*To Angie*) You – taking you. Or he *thinks* he is. But he has me to bypass first.

Angie I wouldn't mind going to London with him – if he'd asked me. But he never asked me. All Denny wants these days, if what his sister Molly was telling me is right, is to sit in his room reading a book.

A laugh from Paddy

Dicko And? And?

Angie And, Dicko, you're up the wrong tree. Like you've been up the wrong tree half your life.

Dicko (*Indicating Denny*) You're – you're not going with him?

Angie No.

Dicko (*Looking at Denny*) Oh. Well. Well – that's all right then. So: all this talk of going –

Angie Yes: I'm going, Dicko. I'm leaving the town.

Dicko On your own? And to go where? Dublin? London? New York? You haven't it in you to go to London, Dublin, anywhere, on your own. I know you. (*A smirk comes on his face*) Know you better than any of them here realize.

Angie Thank you, Dicko. There's a real man talking.

Dicko I'm a real man all right – where you're concerned, miss. That brought me knowledge of you like nothing else could. And I know you'd never go on your own.

Angie I'm *not* going on my own.

Dicko You said – (*Indicating Denny*) Him. That guy.

Angie Oh, Dicko, I can't talk with them all listening.

Denny (*Moving*) I'm off anyway.

Liam (*Moving*) And we'll move too. Peg –

Dicko No: stay! (*To Angie*) Say what you have to say. These people can hear. They're our people. Our neighbours. Out with it.

Peg Will *I* tell him, Angie?

Angie (*Turning away slightly*) You tell him, Peg.

Peg (*Walking over to Dicko*) She's leaving the town, Dicko, with Maguire. He asked her to marry him last night. She said yes. She told me on the way down here. She's been trying all day to find a quiet five minutes on her own with you to tell you.

Dicko (*Looking at Angie, who is turned away from him. He is barely able to speak with surprise*) Maguire?

Angie (*Quietly: still turned away*) Yes.

Paddy (*Taken aback too*) Maguire? (*Then, after a pause*) Oh – ho! (*A little laugh*) Anyone with eyes in his head could see that coming.

Dicko (*To Angie*) Th' Orangeman?

Angie I'm going up to Newry with him. He's fixed a job there.

We're leaving the minute Reikharts shuts. I was looking for you to tell you. I wanted to see you on your own – to say – I suppose – goodbye.

Liam He'll go places, Maguire.

Dicko Angie you'll be lost outside the town. (*A little laugh*) But – you're – are you – ? Ah, go on – you are!

Angie What?

Dicko You're trying it on. That's it, isn't it? Trying a bluff. To get me to do what you want.

Angie I don't want you to do anything, Dicko. Not for me, anyway. I want you to do things for yourself. Don't go on the dole, for a start, spending your days pitch-and-tossing down here. Get a job. If it's not possible here, go some place where it is possible. But for me – no, there's nothing you can do for me any more.

Dicko Yes, I can. You and me.

Angie No, Dicko.

Dicko I won't bloody hear no. Fuck Maguire.

Angie It's over, Dicko.

Dicko Never over. Never! The town knows. Peg there – and Liam – isn't that right, Peg, right, Liam? They know. And Paddy – am I not speaking the truth, Paddy? They all know. Yourself and myself, Angie. School kids together. Us two.

Angie Once maybe. That's gone. We said goodbye a long time ago.

Dicko What, for Christ sake, you on about? We never said goodbye. We had rows – barneys – sure – plenty, plenty – who doesn't? But –

Angie Dicko: I hate it like this in front of them all.

Peg Go down the river for a walk, the two of you. Talk between yourselves.

Angie No, Peg, I'm going home.

Dicko I'll come too. Peg's right. We'll talk. (*Suddenly loud*) All right, I'll – I'll go with you. You just say: Dublin, London wherever. We'll – aye – we'll marry. If that's what you want. Here or some place else. Whatever. You say. (*A loud cry*) I'm fucked without you, Angie. (*Quieter*) I'll – I'll go along with it – whatever you want. Aye, you're right – the dole – nothing here – a fucking washout – I will – but you have to be with me, Angie – you have to be there.

Angie (*Quietly*) I was there far too long, Dicko. I'm there no more. I'm going home now. I've – I've things to do.

She moves towards path R. Paddy takes a step down to her.

Paddy So it's Maguire, eh?

Angie (*Stopping*) It is.

Paddy Aye. (*Slight pause*) You'd – you'd never – I suppose –

Angie (*Turning to Paddy*) Never what, Paddy? I won't hear anything against Maguire.

Paddy No – nothing against him. But you'd never – would you – see if he'd sound out – ?

Liam (*Coming forward*) Sound out Van Druthen. That's it, isn't it, Paddy? Say – the workers might be prepared to take a cut. Isn't that your idea, Paddy?

Angie (*Hardly believing what she has heard*) You'd take a cut, Paddy?

Paddy The jobs are needed.

Dicko A cut! Good man, Paddy. I knew you'd come up with something. Aye, aye: a cut! We'd take it: the jobs'd be saved. (*To Angie*) Your job'd be saved. You'd stay in the town. Things'd – go on.

Angie No, Dicko. Things can't go on.

Paddy (*To Angie*) Get your sweet tongue working. Use it on Maguire.

Angie My sweet tongue might have worked a few months ago when Maguire was urging you, Paddy, and the rest of us to back him. But the only word to come out of our mouths at that time was: No! No, no, to every positive way forward. And that would be Maguire's answer now if I put your suggestion to him. A loud – No! He's washed his hands of this place. And I think I've washed my hands of it too.

Paddy (*Moving away with a sneery laugh*) Aye, you could do with a good wash!

Angie After talking to you for five minutes, I always feel I could, Paddy.

Paddy Whoring round every male in the vicinity. The sooner we're shut of the likes of you in the town the better for us all. You and your immoral goings-on do not belong here.

Angie You're right, Paddy, I don't think they do.

Paddy (*Turning to Dicko*) We'll go over the road, Dicko. It'll be whiskey tonight.

Dicko Whiskey, Paddy?

Paddy Whiskey. To celebrate your near escape from – (*Indicates Angie*) this low tart.

Dicko (*To Angie*) Angie –

Angie Go on, Dicko, your pal needs you.

Paddy He does. And, by jaysus, his pal'll give him something *you* could never give him.

Angie That's very true, Paddy.

Paddy (*To Dicko*) Come on, th' man! Get out of the putrid atmosphere this hoor generates. (*Paddy and Dicko walk a few steps towards the bank L. Paddy puts his hand on Dicko's arm: they stop*) And, d'you think, Dicko, that Maguire is aware of the fact that you were a real man, as far as her ladyship is concerned?

Liam Ah, now, now, –

Peg Don't make trouble, Paddy.

Paddy (*To Dicko*) It might be something he'd be interested to know, would you not think so?

Angie And you'd be the man to tell him, wouldn't you, Paddy? Although, I doubt you'd tell him to his face. However, I'll inform him that you wish to have a chat with him. O.K.?

Paddy Come on, Dicko. Never forget the turned back. That's all that's good for her sort. You're joining us, Liammy?

Peg Go on, Liam. Have your drink. I'll be off home in a minute.

Paddy (*Laughing*) Home! The loyal wife goes back to her family fireside! But there's a slight distraction here before she resumes her domestic duties, eh, lads? (*Laughs: then, shouting across to Denny*) Goodbye, the exile! With your big success in the great metropolis across the water! Carry on the good work.

Denny (*Smiling*) I'll try, Paddy.

Paddy (*Laughing*) Begod, wasn't it the big mistake the rest of us made not going off to London all them years ago to be the great men we could have become like the great man you've become!

Denny (*Smiling: quietly*) Goodbye, Paddy.

Paddy (*Laughing: to Denny*) Send us a few tips in the post about how to be the big success. (*Going off over the bank laughing*) We'll all maybe have a go at it one of these fine days.

Paddy goes off laughing. Dicko looks at Angie, not sure whether to leave or not.

Dicko (*Slowly to Angie*) You unfaithful – after all we – the two of us – after all that – you –

He shakes his head, turns, and follows Paddy off. Pause.

Liam (*Shaking hands with Denny*) Goodbye, Denny.

Denny Goodbye, Liam.

Liam There'll be a day again. There will.

Denny I'm sure there will, Liam.

Liam Good luck, Angie.

Angie Thanks, Liam.

Liam Maguire'll do all right.

Angie If he doesn't, it's a bad look out for the two of us.

Liam You'll be all right. I'll – I'll be home in a short while, Peg.

Peg I will too, Liam.

Liam (*Looking at Peg, then at Denny*) Aye. (*He goes off L*)

Angie Well, Denny, it's been nice meeting you. If I'd come on the scene earlier than I did or if you'd been round a few years later – but there – who can say?

Denny Goodbye, Angie. Good luck up in Newry.

Angie Thanks. I don't know what it's like. But then I don't know what any place is like beyond the main street of Tullamore. I'm going to have to throw off the small specs I've worn in this town. D'you think I'll manage?

Denny You'll manage, Angie.

Angie Aye, maybe I will. (*Slight pause*)

Denny I think you've picked the right man.

Angie I don't think I've picked the wrong one. (*Shaking hands with Denny*) Good luck.

Denny Good luck, Angie.

Angie I'll be seeing you, Peg.

Peg See you, Angie. (*Angie goes off R. Pause*) So, Denny: you're off.

Denny In the morning.

Peg And Angie's off: with Maguire. All going. (*Slight pause*) And what's this about you and your books?

Denny (*Laughing quietly*) Oh, it's no big deal. It's what I like to do these days. And – I – I go to evening classes in London. You know – writers and the stuff they wrote.

Peg No surprise there! That was you from day one.

Denny (*Smiling*) So you said. (*Pause: moving*) Well –

Peg (*Moving quickly to him*) No, don't go, Denny. Not yet. Stay just a minute. I'd like to talk. We haven't talked for – (*He sits on the stump of tree. A pause. Peg walks around*) Angie going. She's – you know – twittery, gets on my nerves at times. But she brings a bit of life to the place.

Denny I can see that.

Peg A bit of – oh, what it was like to be young. (*Pause*) Your mother – that was sad.

Denny It was.

Peg When I heard the news – it was like a death in my own family. She was such a lovely woman. Lived for the day when she'd see you again. (*A quick burst*) And you couldn't find the time to come back and visit her – you were too busy over in England with your – your (*Quieter*) Sorry, maybe I shouldn't be saying this. But I feel I can say things to you, as no one else can. (*Pause*) No: I can't understand you, Denny, honest to God, I can't. How could you cut yourself off like that? (*Suddenly emotional*) You know, you're a selfish bastard. You have to get away from the town, you have to fulfil yourself – your books – your evening classes – But there are other people too – other people's lives you touch – you know – there's – there's – (*She puts her fists to her mouth: she is near to breakdown. Pause*)

Denny (*Quietly*) Yeah – well –

Pause. She moves away from him.

Peg God, this pitch-and-toss spot is a depressing hole. (*She looks up suddenly at him*) You're not off yet? Please: just another minute. (*Slight pause*) I wouldn't blame you if you did want to be off – all the things I've said to you. It's really none of my – well, yes, it is my business. Anything to do with you is my business. Is that an awful thing to say? I'm the wife of another man, the mother of his two sons and I say you're still my business. And maybe –

Denny Maybe what?

Peg Maybe it's all my fault. If I'd done, as you wanted me to, if we'd – you know – us – London – wherever – They say some things are meant to be. Maybe we were meant from the moment of birth to be together.

Denny Maybe is a shaky word, Peg.

Peg I tell myself that. I tell myself we should – well, forget the past and look to the future.

Denny Your sons are the future.

Peg If they are, God help the future. Two big lumps of eating machines. Shovelling chips and steak down their gullets morning and night. (*Slight pause*) Aye, my dear lads: that's what I got. And you got – well, I'm not sure what *you* got, Denny. You got a clean break from this town. It was what you wanted.

Denny I thought it was.

Peg Yeh. (*Pause*) God: I've gone on, haven't I? All come out in the soap suds, as we used to say. Might as well let the rest of it out while I'm at it. So here it is. (*Speaking very quietly*) It's all still there, Denny, not a scrap, not a wisp of it changed. I know it's not the same for you. I know it isn't. I just don't want to hear you say it isn't. Please don't say it. (*Silence: she waits. then, quietly*) No. (*Slight pause*) I'm glad you didn't say It. (*Pause*) So: writers and the stuff they wrote, eh? (*He smiles*) D'you know – once – not out by the river – we were walking out the Birr road – you said a bit of poetry for me – poetry that's forever stuck in my head – about – well, I may as well say what it was about – it was about the end of love.

Denny (*A little laugh*) Not an uncommon subject for a poem!

Peg No more walking – for the boy and the girl or – no more roaming –

Denny Oh! (*Slight pause*) We'll go no more a roving.

Peg That's it – that's the one! Going no more a roving. I thought at the time that could never happen to us. That happening to you and me seemed as unlikely as the sky falling in. But – there you are. (*Slight pause*) D'you remember that poem, Denny?

Denny I do

Peg Would – would you say it for me now?

Denny Oh, I don't know, Peg. My poetry spouting days are long gone.

Peg Mine haven't even begun. Please – like when we used to walk out the Birr road and walking down the river.

Denny Well – (*Pause*)
So we'll go no more a-roving,
So late into the night,
Though the heart be still as loving
And the moon be still as bright. (*He stops*)

Peg If there's more, I'd like to hear it.

Denny Though the night was made for loving
And the day returns too soon,
Yet we'll go no more a-roving,
By the light of the moon.

Peg It's sad, isn't it? Going no more a-roving. Is it Yeats?

Denny No: Byron.

Peg Byron, is it? I suppose you studied that at your evening classes?

Denny That. And Shelley: Wordsworth too. Yeats, Eliot.

Peg You were going to write a poem for me once.

Denny (*Surprised*) I was what?

Peg I asked you to write me a poem. Out by the lake one Sunday.

Denny I never remember you asking me to write a poem.

Peg Oh, I did. You were going to write lots of poems – oceans of poetry. You see, Denny, I knew you better than you thought. I knew what lit the fuse of your discontent with Reikharts and with your life here.

Denny Hindsight, Peg.

Peg No hindsight. Insight. I knew the dream at the heart of it all: the stories you'd write, the poems. And I knew too you felt you couldn't do it if you had this town hanging out of you.

Denny (*Moving*) Look, Peg –

Peg But I never thought you'd take it that far: abandon the town, yes, but to abandon everything else too. Even your mother. Jesus, that was a terrible thing to do, Denny. I mean I was – well, after all, I was only the girl that worshipped the ground you walked on – I was nothing – but your mother, for God's sake –

Denny I have to –

Peg Well, you went, you got away, put miles between the lot of us. And you did – what? Where are the – ? You know. Where, eh? All the things you were going to write?

Denny (*Walking a few steps*) Peg –

Peg (*Loud: angry*) Where, Denny? Show them to me. Show me you went and *did* something. Besides throwing away good chances of super jobs and not making a go of your marriage. And leaving me to struggle for breath in this town. Can you show me anything?

Denny (*Quietly*) No.

Each line builds to a climax.

Peg Nothing? No book?

Denny (*A little louder*) No.

Peg A few words on a printed page?

Denny No.

Peg Not even scraps or bits from a newspaper?

Denny (*Quite loud*) No.

Peg (*Very loud*) Why? Why not?

Denny (*Very loud*) For the simple reason I can't do it. (*Long pause. Then he speaks more quietly*) I cannot do it. (*Pause*) All that: that long trail from here to England, from Reikharts to managing the shoe shop in London, through other jobs, marriage, night classes and a million and one things, was all to come face to face with that discovery: I cannot do it. I never could. I do not possess the knack, the facility, skill or trick, the – whatever it is – the God given thing, no amount of hard work, training or dedication can bring about. I was not in the queue the day they dished out that particular gift. I thought I was. I wasn't. I was in another queue altogether. They awarded me expertise in things I don't give a damn about. (*Slight pause*) So Paddy and the lads were more right than they knew: I didn't reach the goal I was aiming at going to London. They were right to mock.

Peg (*With feeling*) They were not!

Denny Yes: they were. They hit the mark, sure enough. They just didn't know how dead on the bull's eye they really were. Sitting long hours in a chair in a single bleak North London room, pen held over empty page, it at last came to me: I was chasing after a thing that was never there. That never *had* been there.

Peg (*A pause*) So: it was all for nothing.

Denny Nearly nothing. Not quite. I did achieve the feat of getting away from here. Even though here has never quite got away from me. And through the night classes, which were originally intended to help me into the writing, I learned how to read. It's not the greatest thing to have achieved, not the ambition that sets you alight and puts your brain in a spin when you're twenty one. But it's a thing I'm pleased to have discovered, content to settle for these days. It isn't what I was looking for. But it's what I found. I'm happy with that.

Peg Happy? Is that the right word to use?

Denny Maybe happy is a word we should never use.

Peg I use it. I use it about the time you and me wandered down the river. You — your poems — us together. That, for me, is the definition of that word, the word happy. It's sad to say it, but I can live these days because I once had that. (*Pause. She listens*) Listen. Is — is that the lads coming back from Hickeys?

Denny (*Walking up the bank, looking off L*) Hickeys. Time has come up against a red traffic light in that dusky corner of our native earth. Cock your ear and you can hear them in the distance: their talk, football, politics, the dirty jokes, farm chat. (*Turning, coming back down the bank*) And yet you can still hear the birdsong in the trees and the call of the wild fowl (*Nodding his head towards R*) beyond on the lake or down the river. Hickeys hasn't managed to drown that out. It's the one thing I feel at ease with here: the song of the birds and the cry of the geese out over the lake.

Peg Don't you feel at ease with me?

Denny Do the stars feel at ease in the sky?

Peg The stars at ease in the sky. That's nice. Sort of like a poem. Maybe you *will* write poems one day, Denny.

Sheil appears on the bank L.

Sheil (*Brightly: waving*) Hello.

Peg (*Turning*) Sheil!

Sheil (*Coming down to Peg*) Hello, Peg. How are you, Peg?

Peg I'm all right, Sheil. How are you?

Sheil I'm great, Peg, great. I haven't seen you this long while. You're busy of course. Liam. Your boys. A wife's life is a busy life. A married woman in her own lovely house. Getting things all nice and lovely for her husband. Dressing up nice and smart to be going beside him to Mass Sunday. The two of you walking down the town: Peg and her husband. And her two lovely − (*She has been walking around, eyes on ground, occasionally looking up at Peg. Now she looks up and is face to face with Denny up to now she hasn't noticed him*) Is it − ? It is! Isn't it, Peg?

Peg   It is, Sheil.

Sheil   Denny.

Denny   Hello, Sheila.

Sheil Sheila. No one has called me Sheila in years. I love to be called by that name. Thank you, Denny.

Denny How are you?

Sheil I am very well, thank God, Denny. How are *you*?

Denny I'm well too.

Sheil You were away, weren't you?

Denny I was.

Sheil And you're back now?

Peg No, Sheil, he's −

Sheil On a holiday, is it? It's nice to come home for a holiday, Denny. Especially this time of the year. Down the river it's lovely now. And out by the lake. Where is it you are?

Denny England.

Sheil Are you, now? There's lots from here in England. I was never in England. The furthest I've ever been is Dublin. Dublin seemed a great place when I was a girl. We were always going to Dublin, mam and daddy and me. Tea in Bewleys in Grafton Street. And the big cream buns. And the pantomime in the Gaiety. Nearly every Christmas we'd drive up for it. Dublin! In by Inchicore we'd go. Daddy always used to say when we were driving to Dublin, he'd say: We'll go in by Inchicore. I don't know why he always said that, Denny, for we never went in by any other way. There is no other way to go in to Dublin from here but by Inchicore, is there?

Denny I don't know. Sheila.

Sheil I don't think there is. The road to Inchicore. That's the way the trip to Dublin always sounded inside my head: taking the road to Inchicore. (*Slight pause*) I thought one day I maybe might take it for good. Go in by Inchicore, get a good job, a nice flat in Dublin. A man I'd marry. (*Slight pause*) I never did.

Peg (*After a pause*) Sheil: d'you want me to walk you home?

Sheil (*Not having heard Peg: moving around*) It's a lovely evening, isn't it? The air so fresh. (*Big sniff*) Mmm! Perfect! I adore it down the river on an evening like this. And walking out the fringe of lake.

I never cared for this place here, the pitch-and-toss green. But the banks by the river, the soft grass, water lapping the stones. Lovely. A boy and a girl together. A boy and a girl in love. (*Turning to them*) Like the two of you: Peg and Denny. Real love. You're such a lovely couple. I see you down the river most nights, hand in hand, lying together on the grass, kissing. I love looking at the two of you. Made for each other: everyone says that. Peg and Denny. And one day, please God, you'll get married and live in a nice house and have lovely children.

Peg (*Taking a step to her*) Sheil –

Sheil Your mother died, Denny. That was sad. Your mother was a real lady. All the Kerry toffees she used to sell us in her shop. Why do people die, Denny?

Denny I –

Sheil (*Pointing*) There's a dark cloud over there. Look: there. I don't like dark clouds. It might rain down the river tonight.

Peg I'll take you home, Sheil.

Sheil moves away from Peg and suddenly starts to sing.

Sheil Down by the salley gardens my love and I did meet,
She passed the salley gardens with little snow white feet,
She bid me take love easy, as the leaves grow on the tree,
But I, being young and foolish, with her would not agree.
Miss Higgins taught us that in school, didn't she, Peg? (*Turning to Denny*) You said poetry for us down the river, Denny, one Sunday. D'you remember? You said poetry for Peg, myself and Margaret McConnell. Red Flame McConnell we called her. Because of her flaming red hair. She's dead now.

Peg She's not, Sheil. She's married in Canada with three children.

Sheil Married with three children? Oh, isn't that lovely! We were sitting on the grass, Denny. Red Flame beside me. Peg with you, of course. And you said the poems for us.

Denny I forget that, Sheila.

Sheil Oh, I like you calling me Sheila. Sheila's my name. But, sure, that was you always, Denny. Poems and writing and all. You could think of nothing else. You'd put us all in a book one day, we knew you would.

Denny (*Taken aback*) What?

Sheil We'd be in your stories and they'd be printed for all to read. You'd be the boy to do it: that was certain. And I'm so pleased you went away and did the thing you wanted to do. It must be lovely to be able to write things down like that: all that poetry and stories about people and things that happen. Good on you, Denny, you were the man for that. Isn't he great, Peg?

Denny Well, now, Sheila, d'you see –

Peg (*Coming in very quickly*) He is, Sheil. Great.

Sheil (*Singing*) In a field by the river my love and I did stand,
And on my leaning shoulder she laid her snow-white hand,

She bid me take life easy – ah – she – ah – bid me – ah –
she bid me – take – take – life easy – ah – (*Pause*)

Denny (*Singing very quietly*) – as the grass grows on the weirs –

Sheil Aye, Denny, that's it: (*Singing*) – as the grass grows on the
weirs –

Peg (*Quietly: speaking*) But I was young and foolish and now am full
of tears.

Sheil (*Swinging round to Peg*) You know that poem too, Peg. 'Course
you do: we said it in school today for Miss Higgins. (*Pause*) But
what are you doing here, Peg? (*To Denny*) And Denny? This is the
pitch-and-toss green. The lads meet here. (*She picks up the pitch-
and-toss stone*) This is their stone, (*She drops it, recoiling from it, as if it
were dirty*) I don't like that stone. (*To Denny*) You and Peg shouldn't
be here, Denny. You should be walking Peg down the river. (*Then
she goes to Denny, puts her hand to his face*) Are you all right, Denny?
You don't look well. You should take care of yourself. Look after
the health, Denny. You have to keep yourself well for Peg. (*She
turns away from him*) Well, all the best. 'Bye, Peg. (*She walks up the
bank L*)

Peg 'Bye, Sheil.

Sheil I might see the both of you down the river later on. If it
doesn't come on to rain. (*She stops, turns to Denny*) Oh, I forgot to
say how sorry I was to hear your mother died, Denny. That was
sad. Yes, I think that was very sad.

Sheil goes out. Pause.

Peg (*Walking up the bank, looking after Sheil*) Oh, God, Denny.

Denny That's Sheila?

Peg (*Turning to Denny*) Denny.

Denny She was a grand girl.

Peg What's to be done?

Denny I remember her – long hair swinging – at the dances.

Peg Don't go.

Denny And racing and laughing through the town.

Peg (*Coming down to him*) Don't leave me.

Denny Sheila: the loveliest girl.

Peg Stay.

Denny Wha – ?

Peg Don't –

Denny I've got to get back, Peg. The job –

Peg I know – your job – your evening classes – and cutting yourself
off from the town – think I understand – your mother too – she
sees it all now, Denny – sees everything now –

Denny (*Making a move*) Yes. Well –

Peg No, please, Denny. You mustn't. You can't go. Please.

Denny (*Moving*) I told Molly I'd be –

Peg Please – and – yes – d'you think – I might – yes – might like it
in London. I'd – I'd work in a hotel – or in a bar – or cook maybe

for someone – I'm a great cook – you'd – you'd find me a job, Denny – I'd get a room – you wouldn't have to – no, you wouldn't – you could show me London – (*She moves close to him*)

Denny No, Peg.

Peg Please. Don't. You can't. Here – leave me here – no – not that – you can't do that – (*She clings to him, sobbing*)

Denny Peg –

She clings to him. She is crying. After a pause, Liam appears on the bank L. He looks at them, then he walks calmly over to them. He untangles Peg's arms from around Denny's neck.

Liam (*Quietly*) Come on, Peg.

Peg sobs: she clings to Denny

We'll go home.

Liam releases her arms, puts his arm around her, supports her. They walk a few steps.

Have a cry. That's it. Have a good cry.

Liam turns to Denny

She'll be all right, Denny.

Denny She will, Liam.

Liam (*To Peg*) You'll be all right. You will. The summer's still young. We'll have days out. Days with the boys. Days with ourselves. (*Peg turns into him, leans her face on his shoulder, sobbing. He enfolds her in his arms*) We'll go down Wicklow. Go to the sea. We'll walk the strand out at Courtown. Or we'll go away to the west, have a day in Galway and Salthill. We'll take picnics. The weather, they say, 'll be great for the rest of the month. Sure, what does it matter the factory shutting? It's not the end of life. It's not the end of us, Peg. Aye, we'll have a day over Galway and the sea. You'd like that. (*Pause: Liam turns to Denny*) She'll be fine, Denny. She'll be fine. (*To Peg*) Come on. We'll go home now.

Peg (*Walking, Liam's arm around her, speaking as if in a daze*) . . . in that way . . . by Inchicore . . . we'll take . . . take . . . the road to Inchicore . . .

Liam (*Going off R*) We will. We'll do that. If that's what you want. That's what we'll do. We'll take that road. The road to – That's the road we'll take.

They go. Denny looks after them for a long while. Then he turns, looks down at the pitch-and-toss stone, picks it up, turns it in his hands and, after a while, lets it fall to the ground. He takes a look around the green, then walks off slowly R. Long pause. The voice of Paddy is heard singing "The Rose of Tralee" drunkenly in the distance. The stage is empty. Paddy's drunken singing is heard in the distance. Then Sheil comes on L. She walks to the centre and is turned away from the singing. She stands very still. She then becomes aware of the singing and she turns towards it. There is a pause in the singing and in the pause Sheil says her line.

Sheil (*Submissively speaking towards where the singing is coming from*) Sheil's here, Paddy. Did you call, dear? Sheil's here.

The singing starts again. Now Dicko's voice joins Paddy in the singing. The lights fade very slowly with Sheil standing centre looking off L. Paddy and Dicko's drunken singing is still heard in the distance. The lights fade to darkness.

THE LONG ROAD TO DUBLIN

Characters

Liz
Willie
Tom
Jim
Liam
The Sergeant

The play takes place in the kitchen of a farmhouse in County Westmeath. The year is 1958.

AGES: Liz, Willie, Jim and Liam are in their late thirties. Tom is about seventy. The Sergeant is about fifty.

All the songs were popular around 1958.

ACT ONE

Scene One

Liz is working in the kitchen. The radio plays "Volare", sung by Dean Martin. Liz hums with the tune. After a while Willie appears at the door UL. He carries a bulky hold all. Liz doesn't see him. He watches Liz working. After a few seconds he speaks.

Willie Nice tune.
Liz (*Turning*) God!
Willie Door was open.
Liz I leave it open.
Willie Shocked you.
Liz Fright. Yeah, you –
Willie Sorry.
Liz Gave me a –
Willie Apologies.
Liz (*Turning down the radio*) What do you – ?
Willie Should have knocked.
Liz You should.
Willie Should.
Liz Who are you?
Willie Nobody.
Liz Nobody?
Willie In the sense that it would mean anything to you.
Liz In the sense that what would mean anything to me?
Willie In the sense that who I am would mean anything to you.
Liz You're not a local. What do you want?
Willie A train, a bus.
Liz There's no train or bus here.
Willie No, I noticed it didn't say train station as I came in.
Liz It didn't say farm either. But that's what it is.
Willie Your farm?
Liz My father's farm. One day it will be mine. We haven't sorted it out properly yet.
Willie I should sort it out properly.
Liz You walk in here and, within a minute, tell me what to do about my private affairs.

Willie Maybe you could tell me what to do about my private affairs.

Liz I know nothing about your private affairs.

Willie You know I want a train or a bus.

Liz There's no train or bus. We're in the middle of the country.

Willie It has been known for trains and buses to run through the middle of the country.

Liz You don't know *this* middle of the country.

Willie I know it's beside the main road.

Liz The main Galway Dublin road.

Willie I was dropped off on the main Galway Dublin road.

Liz Who dropped you off?

Willie A friend.

Liz Not much of a friend if he dropped you off in the middle of nowhere.

Willie Is this the middle of nowhere?

Liz Most times it seems like it.

Willie Whatever it seems like, it's here I was dropped off. My friend was going south.

Liz You're not going south?

Willie I'm going east – back to Dublin.

Liz It's a long road to Dublin.

Willie I need a train or bus to travel that long road.

Liz There's a bus in town. But that goes tomorrow morning. You might get a train.

Willie In the town?

Liz Yes.

Willie Where is the town?

Liz (*Pointing*) Six miles that way. But I'm not sure – I don't know about trains. And – and sorry, but it isn't every day a strange man walks in my kitchen. I think you should be on your way now.

Willie (*Moving*) I will. Sorry I disturbed you.

Liz Well – a man I never seen before. What d'you expect?

Willie Goodbye.

Liz Goodbye. (*He leaves. She looks through the window*)

Willie (*Reappearing at the door*) Ah – which way did you say the town was?

Liz (*Pointing*) That way.

Willie Thank you. Again – goodbye.

Liz Goodbye, again. (*He starts to go*) If my father was here –

Willie (*Stopping*) Yes?

Liz He might drive you to town.

Willie He sounds a kind man.

Liz Well – he'd look kindly on a tourist stranded. But he's not here, so you'd best get going.

Willie I'm going. But – I'm not a tourist.

Liz What *are* you?

Willie Does it matter?

Liz It matters. People we know nothing about don't walk in our kitchen every day of the week.

Willie An eminently respectable person walked in your kitchen.

Liz You don't look particularly eminent or respectable. And I've tons of work in front of me. So be off with you. It's a job and a half looking after two men.

Willie Your father?

Liz My father.

Willie And – ?

Liz And – the other one.

Willie Your brother?

Liz No.

Willie I saw him, did I not? In the field there at the side as I came in?

Liz You might have.

Willie He lives here?

Liz None of your business. Get off to town.

Willie I will: your workman is none of my business.

Liz He's not my workman.

Willie A relation?

Liz He'd like to be.

Willie A mystery man.

Liz A mystery to you. Off you go now.

Willie (*Moving*) I'm off.

Liz His name happens to be Jim.

Willie (*Stopping*) Jim?

Liz Jim.

Jim (*Entering UL*) Yeah, here I am. (*Looking at Willie*) Who the hell's this fellow?

Liz I don't know.

Jim You don't know?

Liz No.

Jim But you talk to him?

Liz That's the civilized thing to do.

Jim (*To Willie*) Who are you?

Liz Jim, don't be so –

Jim So what?

Liz Well – so rude.

Jim Rude? I come in and find you gasbagging with a stranger in off the street –

Willie In off the main Galway Dublin road.

Jim What am I to think?

Willie Well the main Galway Dublin road –

Jim Never mind the main bloody Galway Dublin road! (*To Liz*) Eh? What am I to think?

Liz Think about what?

Jim About you flirt flying with this fellow?

Liz We were talking.

Jim Talking! Talking! You're always talking. Take my eyes off you for one minute and you're talking. And talking with who? Talking with men. After Mass Sundays outside the church – talking! In the shops in the town – men – talking! In Athlone or Mullingar –

Willie A fine town Mullingar.

Jim In shops, out of shops, coffee in a cafe, it's talking –

Willie She talks well.

Jim Talking well with men. Discussions with men. Jokes, laughs with men. And now here, even in our own home –

Liz It's not your home.

Willie (*Surprised, to Liz*) Not?

Liz Not. It's my father's home. It's *my* home.

Jim All but my home. What I put into it here. Where I am most of the day. And what's been agreed between us – me, you, Tom.

Willie Who's Tom?

Jim Her oul' fella.

Liz He does not like being called an oul' fella.

Jim That's what he is, whether he likes it or not.

Liz He's not that old. And I object to you calling him that.

Jim Object away, my lady. I will call him what I like.

Liz (*Voice getting loud*) You will not! Not in his own house.

Jim This house will be our house. *My* house. He'll be out of our way across in the Corner. And it's up to me what I call anyone in this house.

Liz It may never be your house.

Jim It's been agreed.

Liz My father agreed to nothing.

Jim You and me agreed. You can't go back on that. I put too much of myself and my pound notes into this farm for you or your oul' lad to renege on it.

Willie Renege on what?

Jim Mind your own feckin' business.

Liz Don't speak like that to him, Jim.

Jim I speak as I like. I have rights in this house.

Liz Who gave you these rights?

Jim My money I put in here gave them to me. All I put into this place gives me rights. Your bed gives me rights.

Liz (*Low whisper*) Jim: shut up!

Willie (*Backing away*) I'd better be – the train –

Jim The money I shoved your oul' fella's way gives me rights.

Willie (*Moving*) – on the move – you know – the bus or train –

Liz (*To Willie*) Stay where you are.

Jim (*To Willie*) Yeh, on your bloody bike.

Liz (*To Willie*) Stop there.

Jim (*To Liz*) I won't have you tongue wagging with strangers blown in off the road.

Willie No, I came – d'you see –

Liz (*To Willie*) Don't move an inch.

Willie – the – the main Galway Dublin road – dropped me off – a friend –

Liz (*To Willie*) My father will drive you.

Willie I can – no – it's O.K. – walk – you know –

Liz It's six miles to town.

Jim What's he going to town for?

Liz To catch the Dublin train.

Jim The Galway Dublin train?

Willie That'd be the train.

Jim You'll catch no Galway Dublin train tonight. (*To Willie*) You'll have to go to Mullingar or Athlone to get a Galway Dublin train tonight.

Liz (*To Willie*) My father will drive you into Mullingar.

Jim He has time to drive a traveller off the road into Mullingar.

Willie Ah – no – it's all right – I'll –

Jim Wasting money and petrol on a fellow he's never set eyes on.

Liz If he does, that's his business.

Jim It's *my* business. Every penny he wastes is a penny of mine gone. My father used to say – and he was right – only put into the land what you'll get out. Her oul' fella's down now pouring what we got out of the land here into Conlon's till, filling himself with Powers' whiskey.

Liz (*To Willie*) He'll drive you in, don't worry. He'd do a good turn for anyone, my father.

Willie He sounds a very nice man, your father.

Jim You know nothing about her father.

Willie True. Except she said –

Jim Pay no attention to what she says.

Willie – that he would do a good turn for anyone.

Jim Good turn! All his life doing good turns. With the result –

Liz With the result he's a respected man in the parish.

Jim Respected imbibing John Jameson down in Conlon's! (*To Willie*) Will I tell you what the result is?

Liz (*To Willie*) Don't listen to him.

Willie I think – I'll – be making – a move –

Jim The result is he near bankrupted this farm.

Liz (*To Willie*) Ignore him.

Jim Near bankrupted the farm and herself here, till –

Liz (*To Jim*) Be quiet!

Jim – till I stepped in, till I took over.

Willie And you?

Jim Me?

Willie You are – what?

Liz He thinks he's the boss.

Jim All but the boss. My money, my hard graft, my land knowledge, makes me the boss.

Liz (*Sitting*) You're not boss yet.

Willie (*To Liz*) He *will* be boss, is that it?

Liz That may not be it.

Willie (*To Liz*) I'm unclear –

Jim (*To Willie*) Stay unclear. I'm not explaining to a drifter in off the road who I am.

Willie No, no, why should you?

Jim She knows the story.

Willie Story?

Liz There's no story.

Willie Story – whatever – it's your – you two – not my –

Jim Us two – aye. Her father. And her mother.

Liz (*To Jim*) He doesn't want to know any of that.

Willie That's right – it's none of my –

Jim The story – yeah – her mother dying.

Willie (*To Liz*) I'm sorry to hear that.

Liz Leave it, Jim.

Jim If I'd left it, you'd be in a bad way. (*Moving around*) Her mother was the farm woman. Born and reared on this patch of land. Her family goes back generations. Her oul' lad married into this farm. The mother it was kept it going. The farm woman, d'you see. My father and her mother got on famously. Real farm people, you understand.

Willie (*To Jim*) Oh, I see – you're –

Jim The next farm – aye. Her mother died. What happened?

Willie I – I wouldn't know – d'you see – just – dropped off – main Galway Dublin –

Jim I'll tell you what happened.

Willie No – I don't think you should –

Jim This farm took a nosedive. (*Downward sign with his thumb*) Without her mother it was going nowhere land. And what didn't help –

Willie What didn't help?

Liz (*To Willie*) Never mind what didn't help. It's nothing to do with you.

Willie (*To Jim*) I think she's right. Very interesting – yes – but after all – I'm only –

Jim What didn't help was his lordship – the lord of the manor, so to speak – likes (*Mimes a drinking gesture*) th' oul' uisce beatha, making him, not only unsteady on his feet, but unsteady (*Points to his head*) up here too.

Liz My father's a good man. I won't have you speaking of him in that way.

Jim I speak what way I like. (*To Willie*) Because you know why?

Willie Well – as I say – it's none of my –

Jim I'll tell you why.

Willie Please don't.

Jim Because, my friend –

Liz He's not your friend.

Willie No, d'you see, I'm simply –

Jim I speak as I like in this house because she's too far in with me now – or to put it another way – I've been too far into her for her to stop me speaking as I like.

Liz You *would* put it another way, wouldn't you? You'd put it in your low way.

Jim Low way, high way, (*To Willie*) you wish to know why she's so deep in with me?

Willie I'd rather not, if it's all the same to you.

Jim I'll tell you.

Willie I wish you wouldn't.

Jim She was lost here. Th' oul' lad was lost. All their good land was lost.

Willie Fascinating – but – you know – the Dublin train –

Jim It was then –

Willie – Mullingar – the railway station –

Jim I stepped in. The neighbour in to the rescue. Pulled the whole enterprise up. Pulled the daddy up made him cut down on the yellow stuff. (*Indicates Liz*) Pulled her up too.

Liz You think you did.

Jim Oh, bedad, I did. (*To Willie*) An oul' maid descending fast into a sexless spinster. I changed that. I made her into a woman again. D'you know what I did?

Willie I don't. And I'd much prefer to keep it that way.

Jim I took her to my bed.

Liz Jim – please!

Jim Or I should say: I came to her bed.

Willie Oh – so – you and she –

Jim Her and me.

Willie – you're husband and wife?

Liz (*Loud*) No!

Jim Not in the immediate present, as they say. The way of things here – the slow country way – is to marry first and do the bed stuff after. I'm doing the bed stuff first and I'll put the ring on her finger when the right day comes.

Liz That day may never come.

Willie Well – that's a private thing between the two of you. I don't think you should speak of it to a stranger.

Liz (*Quietly*) He shouldn't.

Jim Stranger, neighbour, priest, minister, king or queen, I speak as I want. (*Moving*) I'm going out now. I've work in a far field. You'll not be here when I get back. Understand me?

Willie Clearly.

Jim Get yourself to town or to Mullingar or wherever. But you'll not be here. O.K.?

Willie O.K.

Jim O.K. (*To Liz*) And no gabbing and confabbing with him. D'you hear me? (*Jim moves to the door UL. He gives Willie's holdall a kick.*) And take this with you while you're at it.

He goes. Willie moves to the door.

Liz Where are you off to?

Willie He said –

Liz Never mind what he said. You're going to walk out without a cup of tea, are you? You look a poor bedraggled oinseach on your last legs in need of nourishment. (*She gets the kettle and holds it out to him*) Here, fill this from the pump out in the yard.

He takes the kettle, goes out UL. Liz turns the radio on: it plays "Everybody Loves a Lover", sung by Doris Day.

Liz continues doing housework while the song plays. Willie comes back with the kettle.

Willie Here. (*He gives the kettle to Liz, who puts it on the turf fire*)

Liz Sorry.

Willie Why are you sorry?

Liz Jim.

Willie Your – ?

Liz Yeh.

Willie Neighbour.

Liz You can call him that.

Willie No bother. Worse has been thrown at me. Worry not about me. It's you I'm worried about.

Liz You can't be worried over a person you don't know.

Willie I know what I heard.

Liz You heard too much. A travelling man should not listen to what is said as he passes by. He should ignore what he hears. And get back to Dublin to his life there and his family.

Willie I don't know about a life there. Nor a family.

Liz No family? What is there in Dublin?

Willie Oh – (*Liz turns off the radio*)

Liz I know that "Oh". It means you don't want to tell me. You saw the insides of my life ripped open just now for you to gawp at, but you clam up about yourself when asked a simple question.

Willie Simple questions often turn out to be extremely complex.

Liz Have you a job in Dublin?

Willie I hope so.

Liz Hope isn't much of a job.

Willie You'd make a good detective.

Liz Not much of a one for the little I've got out of you.

Willie Why should you get anything out of me?

Liz I want to know who I'm talking to.

Willie You're talking to a fellow dropped off in the middle of nowhere. Although I have to say the middle of nowhere doesn't look too bad.

Liz It'd look pretty bad if you lived here.

Willie Why bad?

Liz There's little good. A dance Sunday nights in the town. You have to travel to Mullingar or Athlone to see a picture. And if you haven't a car you're jinxed.

Willie So you don't go into a picture in Mullingar or Athlone?

Liz Once upon a time – often. A long time ago.

Willie You drove your father's car?

Liz I don't drive.

Willie Jim drove you?

Liz Very seldom.

Willie You said often.

Liz (*Speaking in a rush*) I was driven in by someone. Yes: someone. Not Jim. Someone. Every Friday night. Regular.

Willie A regular date?

Liz Regular every Friday night. Regular as clockwork. Then –

Willie Then?

Liz Then a drive out the Athlone road after the pictures. The long road home.

Willie Stopping on that long road?

Liz (*A little smile*) Long stop. Hours stopped by the side of that country highway.

Willie And – no stopping now on that highway?

Liz That highway and that stopping are long gone.

Willie It – he – that time –

Liz (*Loud, speaking in a rush*) That time – yes – that time – that happy time –

Willie Happy?

Liz Yes, yes, happy. (*Loud*) I was happy – them Friday nights – Mullingar – the pictures – the long road home – do you know what happy is?

Willie (*Quietly*) I thought I did.

Liz (*Speaking quickly*) Well, there. That's it. That's all. What are you doing walking into my kitchen getting that out of me?

Willie I didn't want to get it out of you.

Liz You questioned me.

Willie You questioned me.

Liz And little good did it do me, for all the information I got. I don't know who you are. I don't know *what* you are. Have you a name?

Willie It would mean nothing to you.

Liz My father will want to know what it is if –

Willie If he drives me into town to the train?

Liz There's no train. You heard Jim.

Willie It'd be hard not to hear Jim.

Liz Hard or not, he said there was no train.

Willie He said there was a train in Mullingar.

Liz My father mightn't get you to Mullingar. Jim was right.

Willie What was he right about?

Liz He was right about my father. He's too fond of the drop.

Willie Jim?

Liz My father. Jim rarely touches a glass. He's an upright man.

Willie He appears very upright.

Liz Where is my father now?

Willie I don't see him here.

Liz He's never here this time of day. He's down in Conlon's.

Willie A well known hostelry, I should imagine?

Liz A stinking, porter stained oul' shebeen. I worry he'll drive the car in a ditch. That's where you might end up in the car with him going for the train.

Willie But I could walk to town for a train. There's one tomorrow, Jim said.

Liz I don't know. Trains and myself are not on speaking terms. Trains go places. I don't. I'm like one of th' oul' rocks out in the field covered with moss. Stuck. Rooted in mud. Here. This place.

Liz goes to the fire, shakes the kettle.

Willie It seems like I'm rooted in mud too. For tonight anyway – if I can't get to the train in Mullingar. Of course I might get a lift to Dublin at the side of the road.

Liz I doubt if they'd offer you a lift. We're wary of strangers here.

Willie You don't seem wary of me.

Liz I'm wary of you all right. I've a strong eye on everything while you're in the house.

Willie You think there's something here I might take?

Liz You might if you wanted it.

Willie (*A little laugh*) There might be something.

Liz If there is, keep your hands off it.

Willie (*Smiling*) I'll try.

Liz So you're stuck till tomorrow. There might be – (*A pause*) but I'd have to ask my father. And before that I'd have to know who you are. I can't offer you anything till I know that.

Willie Who I am?

Liz Yes. You know who *I* am. You've heard more about me in half an hour than my neighbours have heard in half a lifetime.

Willie I didn't ask to hear it.

Liz I'm asking to hear about *you* – now! You might be a murderer slayed his father or a prisoner on the run from the guards.

Willie I might be, but I'm not. (*Pause: he walks about*) Well – you've heard of people sitting?

Liz Sitting? On chairs?

Willie Chairs, stools, plush seats, benches. And watching. Looking. Paying attention.

Liz Paying attention to what?

Willie To other people.

Liz What other people?

Willie People on something raised.

Liz Like on the back of a lorry?

Willie A bit like the back of a lorry.

Liz Giving an election speech?

Willie Sort of.

Liz You're a T.D.?

Willie A T.D. wouldn't be telling a story.

Liz Some T.D.s tell nothing but stories.

Willie These are not T.D. stories.

Liz What kind of stories are they?

Willie All kinds: funny stories, sad stories, tragic stories, witty stories.

Liz I read stories.

Willie These stories are not read. These stories (*Making a big dramatic gesture*) are acted out.

Liz Like in plays?

Willie Exactly like in plays.

Liz Like the St Patrick Players – the dramatic society – in the parochial hall in the town?

Willie Well, I hope not too like the St Patrick Players.

Liz The St Patrick Players did a great drama one time. This fellow was murdered, but by the end we found out he wasn't murdered at all.

Willie Where can I go to see that play?

Liz What has murders in a play to do with you?

Willie Is the murderer in a play really doing a murder?

Liz No, he's only fooling about.

Willie There you have it.

Liz Have what?

Willie What I am.

Liz You're a murderer?

Willie No, I'm the fellow who fools about in a play.

Liz You're – ?

Willie You see standing before you one of that breed, that low company of men and women, who peddle their wares for pennies in great halls and in tiny rat infested shacks up and down the land.

Liz You're an actor?

Willie I confess to that description of this inferior class of mankind.

Liz Paddy Breen's an actor.

Willie Paddy Breen? Do I know him? Has he trodden the Abbey boards or enacted upon the Gate stage?

Liz I don't know whether he's enacted or not. (*Pointing*) He has the farm on the other side of us.

Willie A farm? And his acting?

Liz He does that with the St Patrick Players. He always acts the eejit. Do you act the eejit?

Willie I have been known to – and often off stage as well.

Liz Are you in a dramatic society?

Willie In a way. Except we call it a theatre company. And we get paid.

Liz Jimmy Breen doesn't get paid.

Willie There are occasions when even we do not get paid.

Liz Why not?

Willie Bad business or if the manager turns out to be a crook.

Liz If he's a crook he should be in jail.

Willie Actors think most managers should be in jail.

Liz Not much acting down this way. Unless you joined the St Patrick Players.

Willie It may come to that.

Liz What's an actor doing being dropped off on the road outside?

Willie Long story.

Liz Make it short.

Willie I was on tour with a company. The tour – ah – ended in Sligo.

Liz My Aunt Brid lived in Sligo. My mother's sister. My mother died when I was nineteen.

Willie I'm sorry.

Liz I'm sorry too. I'm still sorry. It's a terrible thing to have your mother die at nineteen. If we hadn't lost her, everything would have been all right. (*Quickly changing*) So – Sligo? When your tour ended, why didn't they take you back to Dublin?

Willie Well – a friend – d'you see – a lift.

Liz A friend gave you a lift?

Willie Yes, he was going south – Limerick way. He dropped me off here.

Liz That sounds to me stupid. To be dropped off in nowhereland when you wanted to get to Dublin.

Willie Yes – but – nice car ride – good talk – I thought – why not? We – we got held up – he was in a hurry – else he'd have dropped me off in town.

Liz And you still have to get to Dublin for your job. When does that start?

Willie Ah – not sure. It's the way, d'you see, with us players.

Liz Players round here means the lads on the football team. Jim was one of them – a local hero fifteen years ago.

Willie That's why you and he – being a local hero – ?

Liz That's *not* why! That sort of why was never there.

Willie But the two of you – ?

Liz (*Loud*) Will you be quiet! Jim – him – me – nothing to do with you!

Willie Of course not.

Liz What *has* to do with you is where you're going to be put up for the night. (*Thinking*) Of course I'd have to ask my father.

Willie I would not expect your father to share his bedroom with me. And yours – I imagine Jim would have a slight objection to that.

Liz I am not inviting you into my bedroom.

Willie No – no – naturally –

Liz (*Suddenly loud and speaking fast*) It's not Jim's bedroom, by the way. My room is my room! He comes – yes – invites himself in for the night – and comes too – sometimes in the middle of the night – if he wakes up and feels the mood is on him – crosses two fields in the dark night because of what he wants.

Willie Well, that's your own affair – I mean –

Liz (*Continuing: upset*) I wake up – he's there in my bed – foostering – his turnip hands clamped on me. (*Very loud*) What is that? Is that affection for a woman? Is that any kind of respect? Tell me what that is, acting man? Do you know what it is?

Willie (*Quietly*) No, I don't know what it is.

Liz (*Loud*) And what's this – you – you – actor – drawing all that out of me? Is that what you do – you acting crowd? Draw us out, so you can act us on the friggin' stage? Will you be able to act that on the stage back in Dublin – what I've just said – that night call I get at two o'clock in the morning?

Willie (*Quietly*) No, I won't act that on the stage.

Liz And anyway, as I said, it's nothing to do with you.

Willie No.

Liz Your concern is your job when you get back to the city – in one of the Dublin theatres. Is it Shakespeare you're going to be in? My father loves all that oul' stuff. (*Pointing*) He has books of it up there on the shelf.

Willie Ah – not Shakespeare. Although I have played in Shakespeare. In fact, if I may make a small boast, the Evening Press said that my Lorenzo in The Merchant of Venice was astonishing for so young an actor.

Liz You're not so young an actor now. And this big job in Dublin –

Willie Yes – yes – new play – new writer –

Liz My father talks about writers. Yeats and that lot. Till sometimes he'd blow your head off with his oul' talk. I often say he should have been a teacher.

Willie Why did he not become a teacher?

Liz He hadn't the schooling. I'm good at figures and reading – that's because he took me through all that when I was little. And he told stories about Cuchullain and Julius Caesar.

Willie He'd have made a good teacher.

Liz He didn't make a good farmer. Jim was right.

Willie It seems Jim is always right.

Liz Daddy married into this farm. It belonged to my mother's people. Daddy was from a family of labouring men. Mammy's parents were dead set against them marrying. But they were in love. They married in the end. Daddy did his share, but it was Mammy ran the farm. Then she died and –

Willie The farm went down?

Liz Yes, down until neighbour Jim came to the rescue. You have to give him that. (*Loud*) Stop standing there: get yourself a cup and saucer. And let's have a bit of music, for God's sake! (*Turns on radio [song: Sinatra "All the Way"]. He gets cup and saucer from the dresser, puts them on the table, Liz prepares to make tea.*)

Willie (*After 30 seconds of song*) So – Jim – the farm – you – ?

Liz What are you talking about? Jim – the farm – me! (*Turns radio off*) What is it to you? That's a story rooted in this place. Your story is another story – your part in a play in a Dublin theatre.

Tom (*Coming in*) What Dublin theatre? I saw Hamlet in a Dublin theatre. Oh, how weary, stale, flat and unreliable seem to me the uses of this world.

Willie Unprofitable.

Tom What?

Willie – flat and unprofitable. Not unreliable.

Tom You're dead right. Unprofitable.

Liz Daddy, this is –

Tom Hello, sir! (*Shaking hands*) Delighted to be introduced to you. Didn't catch your full name.

Liz We don't know his fall name. I don't even know his half name.

Tom Full name, half name, you are welcome in my house, sir. Has the man been given a cup of tea?

Liz The man's been given nothing.

Tom Up girl! Set the kettle going.

Liz (*Shaking the kettle*) I've been trying to get it going for the last half hour.

Tom I had a drink with Paddy Breen in Conlon's.

Liz (*To Willie*) The actor – the farm beyond.

Tom The brother Liam is down from Dublin.

Liz (*Turning: touching her hair*) Liam is down?

Tom He'll be calling over. (*To Willie*) He's a teacher in Dublin.

Liz (*Indicating Willie*) This fellow's on his way to Dublin.

Tom A Dublin man – ha? (*Willie nods*) You have a good face – a wholesome face. These days I come back to my humble homestead to be greeted by a fellow's pinched face that repels the birds in the fields. Have you ever come across that sort of face, young fellow?

Liz He's not that young. And he missed the train to Dublin.

Tom Dublin's fair city! City of Joyce and O'Casey, Swift and Wilde. And the Liffey smell when the tide is out!

Liz He's an actor.

Tom I saw actors in Dublin. F J McCormick at the Abbey. Shakespeare in the Gaiety.

Liz Yeah, yeah, we know! He doesn't want to hear about your time as a messenger boy in Dublin. He wants to hear about where he'll sleep. Could he have the Corner for the night?

Willie The Corner?

Tom It's what we call it. Oh, aye! Shoved in a corner, thrown into an outhouse. You, an actor, would know about roles. Old man role, no longer allowed in his own house.

Liz Of course you are! (*To Willie*) It's a sturdy walled outhouse, we always called the Corner. We're converting it.

Tom Converting me to an oul' useless yoke thrown out to where the cattle slept.

Liz (*To Willie*) Don't listen to him. (*To Tom*) It may never happen. And he's not interested in all that. His mind is on the big part he's going to do in Dublin. (*Liz is busy with cups, milk etc. she and Tom speak very fast until the pause*) His tour ended.

Tom Out of my own house.

Liz In Sligo.

Tom Thrown in the Corner.

Liz A friend gave him a lift.

Tom While her and him.

Liz Dropped him off on the road.

Tom A cow shed.

Liz That's what he's doing here.

Tom That's where they're pushing me.

Liz (*To Tom*) Now you know.

Tom (*To Willie*) Aye: now you know.

Pause.

Willie Yes – yes.

Tom Give him something to eat. He can't exist on Shakespeare.

Willie True: Shakespeare makes a bad sandwich.

Liz (*Loud, in a rush*) And, anyway, it might never happen. Who says it has to happen? Who says that? (*She storms out UL, slamming the door behind her. Pause. Willie is now standing by the radio*)

Tom Turn on the wireless there. She'll hear it through the window. She loves the wireless – it calms her. (*Willie turns on the radio. Song: "Stairway of Love" [Michael Holliday]*) Slice yourself a few cuts of bread. The butter's there, jam if you want it. I'll make the tea. (*During song Willie slices bread etc. Tom makes tea. After the song plays for about half a minute, Tom speaks*) So – your tour ended? (*They sit, eating bread, drinking tea*)

Willie Ah – yes. (*The radio plays quietly behind the dialogue*)

Tom Sligo? My wife had an aunt in Sligo.

Willie Your daughter told me.

Tom Ah! She told you things. She has a big mouth.

Willie A pretty mouth.

Tom Like her mother. The prettiest girl in Westmeath.

Willie West Westmeath.

Tom West of bloody nowhere. But you're bound east. Big part in a play in Dublin?

Willie Well –

Tom I took Marion to a play in Mullingar. Marion was her mother. A love story. Suited us at the time. You've been in love?

Willie (*Quietly*) I have.

Tom You'd know about it then. I loved the girl who had a good farm coming to her. I had damn all coming to me. There's your stage setting, Mr Actor, for when I came a-courting into this house. The ructions, the rows, the orders to clear out and never darken this door again. (*Points to door*)

Willie You *did* darken it. You married Marion.

Tom Not till the old man went to his maker. After that, the mother got frail. A man in the house was needed. It worked. Love works. Did you know that?

Willie (*Quietly*) I used to think it did.

Tom It does, oh, it does. All that was fine. But the farm – I was the worst land man in West Westmeath – or wherever the hell we are. Marion had inherited the know how of it. I did what I was told. And I kept my eyes open. You have to with the neighbour we had that way. (*Pointing*)

Willie Jim is that way.

Tom His oul' fella was that way too. And he would like to've – Oh, yes, I kept my eyes open. She was a pretty woman to the day she died. I knew what he was after. But what he could never understand was that Marion loved me. Love works. Failure turned him bitter – he went a bitter man to his grave. That part of the story had a happy end. The second act, as you might say, is not so happy. The son has opened the door closed against his oul' lad.

Willie Jim and your daughter?

Tom She thinks, d'you see, she has to.

Willie Why would she have to?

Tom Ah – because of his investment in our place. She thinks there's no other way. But surely to God, there has to be another way. To see him in here with her and me shoved out in the Corner – the cattle outhouse – that can't happen, (*Getting upset*) tell me that can't happen.

Willie I don't know, Tom. It's nothing to do – I'm only – dropped off on the road outside – that's all I am.

Liz (*Coming in UL*) There! It's not the Gresham Hotel, but you'll be all right for the night. I've put blankets on the old sofa for you.

Willie Thank you.

Liz Take your bag over. I'll show you where it is.

Willie I'm very grateful to you both for putting me up. (*Willie picks up his bag and comes face to face with Jim at the door. Liz turns off the radio*)

Jim Whoa, there, Jinny! Tighten the reins. Who's being put up?

Liz Himself. In the Corner on the old sofa.

Willie They said I could.

Jim Did *I* say you could?

Willie Ah – no.

Jim No. And I say you can't, my sunshine.

Liz It's only one night.

Jim One night, half a night, no, ma'am! (*To Willie*) No, sir!

Willie Well, if it's awkward –

Jim *Very* awkward.

Tom (*Loud: upset*) It's not awkward! It's not!

Jim (*To Willie*) And do I not recall telling you to be gone from here by the time I got back?

Willie Yes – but – d'you see –

Jim I see very well. And when I say a thing, that thing has meaning. I got this farm back on its feet by saying things that had meaning. Them two say things that have no meaning. Th' oul' fella here lets the John Jameson talk. And herself says things, (*Laughing*) oh, by God, you should hear the things she calls out in the dark of night!

Liz (*Quietly*) Shut up!

Jim (*Laughing*) Oh, she never shuts up in the dark bed night time. The stars themselves hear her howls.

Tom Be quiet! Have you no decency in you?

Jim (*Ignoring him*) But where's the meaning in any of it? Rubbish whiskey talk and dark night love talk do not build up a farm. (*Pointing to his head*) This builds up a farm. And I didn't build up this farm to have a drifter in off the road –

Tom The man is an actor.

Jim Acting the poor mouth, hand out for a bit of help. There was no help here when times were bad. I brought in the help. (*To Willie*) Your sort pull down a place. So – now – go!

Tom He has nowhere to lay his head for the night. You wouldn't have him sleeping in a bloody ditch! There's no luck in throwing a man out on the road.

Liz He's only sleeping one night across in the Corner.

Jim Oh, I'm most concerned he has a good night's sleep. But not here! (*To Willie*) Go!

Liz (*Quietly*) Don't go.

Willie (*Moving*) I think – I better –

Tom (*Quietly*) Stay where you are.

Jim (*To Tom*) Excuse me! I spoke. My word was for him to go.

Tom And my word was for him to stay. Whose name is on this house?

Jim Your name on the house? You'd be out of the house, you'd be on the road if it wasn't for me, even if your name was twenty times on the house.

Tom (*Loud: getting upset*) I am the legal title holder here!

Jim Legal title holder? After what I put in here?

Tom Whatever you put in, the ownership still belongs to me. And if I say this gentleman can stay the night, he stays.

Willie (*Moving*) Ah – well – I think –

Jim He goes! And as for the ownership belonging to you, old man, all I say is – not for much longer.

Tom (*Very upset*) You think I'll drop in my grave, do you, for you in some way to get the place?

Jim (*Calmly to Liz*) Tell him.

Tom Tell me what?

Jim (*To Liz*) Go on! Tell him.

Liz (*Quietly to Tom*) He's been talking about a signed agreement. A – a sort of signing over. If – if –

Jim Not if! When! When her and me –

Tom (*To Liz*) You and him?

Jim Yes! Me and her! When that happens.

Tom Signing over? What signing over? I'm signing over nothing.

Jim Are you not? And you think I'd come in here, tie myself to her, and for you to be still in charge?

Willie (*Moving*) You three – this is your – I'll be on my way.

Liz (*Loudly to Willie*) Sit down!

Jim He'll not sit down. If I say he goes, he will go!

Tom (*Rising*) I will say who goes, who stays. It's my house, my farm!

Jim (*A little laugh*) Your farm? It was your wife's farm.

Tom (*Loud: upset*) Mine – my name on legal paper. I'll – I'll –

Jim You'll do nothing, old man. Your day is done here. You almost ruined this farm, I saved it. And now you have the face to tell me who goes, who stays.

Tom (*Rising*) I'll – I'll –

Jim You'll do nothing! Sit down!

Liz (*Quietly*) Aye, sit down, Daddy. (*Tom sits. Liz speaks quietly to Jim*) And you – get out.

Jim (*Ignoring her*) I've work to do. (*To Willie*) You'll be a sorry gent if I find you still here as night darkens. (*Going*)

Liz (*To Jim*) Excuse me. I said something to you.

Jim (*Stopping, turning, a smile on his face*) I wasn't listening.

Liz (*Quietly*) Listen now. Go. If anyone's day is done here, it's yours. You're finished here. We may be finished too, my father and myself, but we'll go down with some respect for ourselves.

Jim (*Laughing*) You bloody *will* go down without me.

Liz You've informed us of that since the day you stepped in here. You talk as if all is settled. You forget nothing is settled.

Jim Oh, yes – we said – we agreed –

Liz If he doesn't agree (*Indicates Tom*) it means nothing.

Jim (*Laughing*) Him! You said, my lady –

Liz I'm going back on what I said. I'm reneging on everything I agreed.

Jim You can't do that, miss.

Liz I've done it, sir!

Jim My stake here –

Liz You've no stake here any more. No stake in this house, this land, no stake with me. Above all, with me. I was the fool of Westmeath ever to let you near my bed.

Willie (*Moving*) Excuse me – I –

Liz (*Loud to Willie*) Sit down!

Jim You let me near your bed because you were withering into an oul' maid, hungry for sex without a man in sight.

Liz Yes, and you came into my bed and there still wasn't a man in sight. And I'll go on withering – at least, I'll sleep at night.

Jim Ha, it wasn't sleep you wanted.

Liz No, and what I wanted I never got. Love? I've known love. But love was a stranger when I let you touch me.

Tom (*Quietly*) Quiet, Liz, quiet!

Liz (*Loudly*) No, I won't be quiet! (*Pointing at Jim*) Till I know he's gone forever. Forever away from me. Out of my life. Out of this house. This farm. Aye, let it go down the drain. Let us all go down the drain. As long as he's gone forever from us. Then I'll be quiet. (*Pause: she speaks quietly*) Yes, yes, I'll be quiet then. (*She sits*)

Jim (*Laughing to Willie*) Enjoyed that, did you? Good bit of acting that, eh, stage man? Could you do as well as that? We've had it before, we'll have it again. Changes nothing. Like the plays you act in. Great sport for five minutes – then gone! In your plays back in Dublin remember what you saw here today. A big scene. Dramatic! But when the clapping's over, just the same as it always was. Nothing changes, actor man! What's your name, by the way? Do you have a name?

Willie Ah –

Jim (*To Liz*) You let in the wild rover from off the road and you don't know his name! (*Laughing*) Good, begod! (*To Willie*) Well, wandering minstrel with no name, be gone from here when I return. (*Laughing*) Or if not, we'll have the makings of a great friggin' play! A great shaggin' epic! (*Laughing*) I'll look forward to that. By Jaysus, I will!

He goes out laughing. Long pause. All sit still. Liz is crying quietly.

Willie (*Rising*) I'd best – you know – yeah – that'd be best – (*He stands, not moving*)

Tom Oh, yes, saw some great plays in Dublin. Plough and the Stars.

Lights slowly begin to come down.

Song – "Catch a Falling Star" (Perry Como) – Gently in.

Julius Caesar. The Playboy. And that other one – what now was that other one? It was – wasn't it? Aye, it was. That was it. 'Twas – 'twas – aye – aye – that's what it was.

Song fully up. Lights slowly to darkness.

Scene Two

Next morning. Liz and Willie standing on either side of the table.

Willie Jim.

Liz What about Jim?

Willie He said he'd do for me if he finds me still here this morning.

Liz (*Laughing*) And that you'd spent the night on th' oul' sofa in the Corner!

Willie A very comfortable night it was too. Thank you.

Liz Not at all, Mr – Well? We can't have a man with no name in the house. No name men are not welcome down this way.

Willie You and your father gave me a welcome.

Liz Because we took it you have a name.

Willie My name is William.

Liz William what?

Willie Good God, a few years ago I thought that question would be unnecessary.

Liz Why?

Willie Because I thought my name would be on every tongue throughout Ireland.

Liz You dreamed you'd be famous?

Willie We all start out dreaming we'll be famous.

Liz You still might be famous. I'm nobody from the back end of Westmeath. I wouldn't know the most famous man in Dublin even if he was face to face with me.

Willie I'm not the most famous man in Dublin.

Liz Being not the most famous man in Dublin doesn't mean you haven't a second name.

Willie Walsh. William Walsh. Willie to my friends.

Liz Am I your friend?

Willie You've proved a good one so far.

Liz (*Turning away*) Ah, but we've only got so far.

Willie Maybe, too far. (*Moving*) I've outstayed my welcome.

Liz Who said you had?

Willie Jim said I had. And I don't want him to find me still here. I'll walk to town, catch the Dublin train.

Liz My father will drive you in. When he gets up.

Willie But his nibs – I'm fearful of facing him.

Liz Where's your guts?

Willie I left them behind in Sligo.

Liz I can't leave them behind anywhere. I have to face him every day.

Willie Yeh, but you're his – I don't know exactly what.

Liz Yes, you do. I'm his bed mate. I gave up a woman's most precious thing to a clod of Westmeath clay. One time I would never have said such words in front of a strange man.

Willie Why do you say them now?

Liz Because – since last night – I want no chains on the truth.

Willie Since last night?

Liz Last night changed things.

Willie Jim said nothing changes.

Liz Nothing used to change. (*Quietly*) Maybe all changes now.

Willie Why now?

Liz You tell me.

Willie I'm in the dark. About everything here. I just want to get on my horse before he arrives. (*Slight pause*) I presume – ah –

Liz What do you presume?

Willie He didn't arrive in the middle of the night.

Liz He didn't. I knew he wouldn't. After the speech I gave him yesterday he always takes a back seat.

Willie Oh, you've given him that speech before? Yeh, he said nothing changes.

Liz You weren't listening to me. I said last night changed things. I'm getting the house key off him.

Willie That'll change things?

Liz It'll change the night time. The days might change after that. (*Looking out the window*) Oh, God, no!

Willie He's coming?

Liz Passing.

Willie Jim.

Liz No.

Willie Who?

Liz (*Looking out the window*) Coming down the lane. Please God, no, not yet. No – no – he's going on. Calling on Doran's further down. (*Going to door UL, calls*) Daddy, get up, will you! I saw Liam Breen walking past to Doran's. He'll be here on his way back. I want you up when he calls.

Willie Who's Liam Breen?

Liz (*Tidying her hair*) Paddy Breen's brother. Down from Dublin – with his wife. Always calls to see us.

Willie With the wife?

Liz No – ah – the wife doesn't call.

Willie But – why the worry?

Tom (*Coming in wearing shirt and trousers. He is in bare feet*) Morning!

Liz Daddy! Will you look at the sight of you! No boots! And I told you Liam will be calling.

Tom Oh – ho! Liam will be calling! (*To Willie*) Note that, my friend!

Liz He's down the lane to Doran's. He'll be here any minute. Get you boots on. I'll tidy my hair. (*She goes off to her room R.*)

Tom (*Putting on boots, socks*) Her hair! Boots! All must be ship shape for Mr Liam.

Willie What's so special about Mr Liam?

Tom Everything's special about Liam. Or, I should say, everything once was special about him. Lovely lad he was. There were great hopes here in them days. But – he went teaching in Dublin. Married. Anyway – how did you sleep?

Willie Well.

Tom You're welcome over there in the Corner for as long as you want.

Willie Thanks. But I'd better be making for Dublin.

Tom Of course. Your work is there. (*Pause*) It's where they're going to stick me, you know. Across in the Corner.

Willie It's not bad over there. Could be done up nicely. I could give you a few tips. I used to do the sets for the company. Design and paint them.

Tom As well as doing your acting?

Willie Yes. It's all hands to the pumps in a touring company. My – ah – well – one of the actresses – very good she is too – as well as acting she has to look after the costumes. Another actress sorts out the props. I did the sets.

Tom Talented man.

Willie One or two critics in Dublin didn't think I was.

Tom Nothing but bloody critics in this place! (*Pause*) Would you – ah – but you wouldn't.

Willie What?

Tom Stay awhile and do it up for us?

Willie The Corner?

Tom Aye – make it nice. I'd want it nice if I have to end my days there. I'd pay you.

Willie Oh, I don't know, Tom.

Tom Of course – your Dublin job – you have to get back for it. A man has to have ambition in your game.

Willie I had lots of that commodity once.

Tom I only had one ambition. To marry Liz's mother. And to be happy with her. I achieved that.

Willie Liz said you should have been a teacher.

Tom (*Laughing*) Lord, no, I'd have been a terrible teacher. No patience, d'you see. I'd have ended up in the Joy for walloping the little brats.

Willie She said you could have taught Shakespeare.

Tom Pay no heed to her. All that Friends, Romans and Countrymen stuff is not for teaching. It's for listening to and looking at. It's for letting it roll round inside your head. Friends, Romans and Countrymen, lend me your ears –

Willie I come to bury Caesar, not to praise him.

Tom The evil that men do lives after them. The good – the –

Willie The good is oft interred with their bones.

Tom Interred with their bones! Aye, begod, that'll be true of all of us one day. Where all our little ambitions will end up.

Willie It was my ambition once –

Tom To act in Julius Caesar?

Willie I *did* act in Julius Caesar. No: Shylock. Merchant of Venice.

Tom I can see you in it.

Willie Seeing me in it doesn't mean I'll ever do it.

Tom You must keep wanting to do it. Ambition is a great thing. Though ambition not realized can kill a man. There was great ambition here once.

Willie You marrying Liz's mother?

Tom Not that.

Willie Liz?

Tom Yes.

Willie And?

Tom Can you not guess? Why d'you think she's run off to comb her hair?

Willie Because – ?

Tom Because Liam might call.

Willie He was – ? Was he – the pictures in Mullingar every week?

Tom Pictures. Dances. Days out in Dublin. Never saw her so happy.

Willie And that was – this teacher – passed down the road a while ago?

Tom Always calls on the neighbours.

Willie Liz was more than a neighbour? What went wrong?

Tom What makes things go wrong always in this house.

Willie Jim?

Tom He set out to destroy them. Killed their love.

Willie Can you kill love?

Tom Right: you can't.

Willie (*Quietly*) I don't think you can.

Tom And he couldn't either. Never killed their love. But he robbed them of what love could have given them. Like his father before him, he had his eye on this house from a young age. The house and what was in the house. But her eyes were turned in the direction of another neighbour.

Willie Liam?

Tom Yes. They were only children. She'd cross the field to his house, he'd come here. Then the pictures in Mullingar every Friday. Dances and all the rest.

Willie He wanted to be a teacher – was that a problem?

Tom Not at all. She'd have gone with him anywhere he got a school.

Liz (*Voice off*) Daddy, are you respectable?

Tom (*Tying his laces*) I'm respectable, I'm respectable. (*To Willie*) Have to be respectable for Liam!

Willie How was it Jim came between them?

Tom He didn't twig at first. Thought she was his, as if it had been ordained by the Almighty. But when he realized how deep it was between her and Liam, he geared into action. He'd push in and go with them to the pictures and the dances.

Willie Why didn't they tell him to go to hell?

Tom I told him to go further than hell more than once. But Liam wasn't that sort of lad, no nasty push to give Jim the boot. It's hard to say exactly what way it happened. He sort of mowed them down. People can be mowed down in life.

Willie (*Quietly*) They can.

Tom Then Liam went for the teaching and –

Willie Jim moved into his place?

Tom He could never move into Liam's place. But, yes, he – as they say – got his feet under the table here. I know she berates herself night and day about it.

Willie Berates herself? I haven't heard that word in a long time. Berate. It's an old word.

Tom We're not short of old words down this way.

Willie Berate – rated. Shylock was rated.

Tom What?

Willie (*Moving to a space*) Signior Antonio, many a time and oft – ah – In the Rialto you have – you have rated me – ah – About my moneys and my usances.

Tom Go on.

Willie Still have I – Still have I borne it with a patient shrug –

Tom For sufferance is the badge of all our tribe.

Willie You know it.

Tom Bits and scraps of it. (*Tom takes a book from the shelf and leafs through it while talking*) Sufferance is the badge of all our tribe round here all right. They'd think the man from Warwickshire was writing about the poor downtrodden Irish. But the downtrodden Irish have been downtrodden by their Irish neighbours as much as by anyone else.

Willie Fling Shakespeare at your neighbour. (*Declaiming*) You call me misbeliever, cut throat dog – and – and –

Tom (*Reading*) And spit upon my Jewish gaberdine.

Willie That's it! And – and – yes! And all for use of that which is mine own.

Tom (*Reading*) Why, look you –

Willie Why, look you, how you storm! (*He circles, turns towards Liz's door R, comes face to face with Liz, who has come out of her room. She now looks very attractive, hair down, a nice dress on, high heeled shoes*) I would be friends with you – (*He pauses and finishes the line quietly*) – and have your love.

Liz (*Smiling*) What?

Tom (*Holding up the book*) Shakespeare.

Liz (*Laughing to Willie*) You have him off again, have you?

Tom He knows it.

Willie I knew it one time.

Liz (*To Willie*) Where did you do that?

Tom He did it nowhere. It's his ambition.

Liz Ambition for what?

Tom To act the part of Shylock, what else?

Willie Once, yes. Not any more.

Liz If you want to act it, act it.

Willie That's not the way it works.

Liz What way *does* it work?

Willie Someone has to ask you to do it.

Liz If you want to do it, do it. Seems easy to me.

Willie (*Snapping*) Easy to you here in the middle of nowhere!

Tom (*Seeing he is upset*) Leave it now. It's not the St Patrick Players you're talking about.

Liz I never talk about the St Patrick Players. Seeing a few of their boring plays is enough.

Tom Put the kettle on. You'll want to offer Liam a cup of tea when he arrives. (*Liz gets the kettle*)

Willie Sorry.

Liz What are you sorry for?

Willie I shouldn't have snapped at you.

Liz Snap away. You and your Shylock or whatever it is – I couldn't care less about it.

Tom Lovely play – lovely part.

Liz Lovely plays – lovely parts – what the hell use is any of that to us, stuck here in mud and muck?

Tom Well – we don't know.

Liz I know. None of that will help us earn pennies from the land. (*To Willie*) Keep your Shakespeare to yourself. Himself there wasted too much of his time on all that. (*Getting emotional*) That sort of stuff doesn't make spuds grow or put bread on the table.

Tom Spuds growing and bread on the table: that's all we want, is it?

Liz (*Loud*) Yes! That's all we want! There's nothing else!

Jim (*Coming in UL*) What – nothing else?

Liz (*Quietly: turning away*) Never mind.

Jim Coming out of Doran's, his highness almost knocked me down.

Tom (*Mumbling*) Pity he didn't.

Liz Liam?

Jim The great teacher down from Dublin. Regretfully, he can't honour us with a visit today.

Liz (*Disappointed*) What?

Jim Sadly, no. We are to be deprived of that great pleasure. Has to go in to Athlone with the brother Jimmy. Ah, but never mind! He'll call before he goes back, he says.

Liz (*Taking off her shoes*) He's not calling.

Jim Oh, crestfallen, are we? Downhearted – ha? Lovely Liam isn't dropping in. End of the world! And the hair nicely done. The dress, the high heels! All to look pretty for the Dublin teacher. (*To Willie*) What d'you think of that, traveller of the roads?

Willie I think she looks nice.

Jim You think she looks nice! Who bloody asked you?

Willie You did.

Jim I did and I see you're still here – what?

Willie I appear to be.

Jim (*Approaching Willie*) And did I tell you not to be here?

Willie Very forcibly.

Jim And very forcibly, here it is again: on your way!

Tom No.

Jim (*Turning to Tom*) What?

Liz No.

Jim What – no?

Liz He doesn't have to go.

Jim Oh, he doesn't have to go! You want him to stay – what? You want another man crawling round you. Paying you attention, giving you compliments and seeing your nice hair, your stylish dress. (*To Willie*) Do you like her pretty hair and her lovely dress, road man?

Willie I think she looks great.

Jim She looks great, does she? And Dublin Liam will think she looks great. He won't see her in boots and an oul' skirt swimming in the mud and the stink of the pigs and the cattle dirt. All the men thinks she looks great in her high heels, men in town, men at Mass, their wives beside them. She wants them to look at her. And at the dances –

Tom What are you talking about? She hasn't been at a dance in years.

Jim I'm not talking to you, old man. Oh, yes, men in shops, men in streets in towns, hair nicely done, all done for the men. Men eyeing her, stripping her clothes off, bed dreaming her. But what did any of them shaggers do for her – ha? Did they pull this land out of poverty? They'd like to do something for her all right, then shag off, buttoning up their trousers.

Tom I refuse to have that sort of dirty talk in this house.

Jim You can refuse what you like. But keep in mind, old man, what I did here for this farm. Put into the land only what you'll get out, my father always said. And he was right. I put in more than my fair share here. And is there a scrap of gratitude for what I done? Is there bollocks! But, by Christ, I'll get out what I put in, I'll get what comes to me by rights.

Willie (*Quietly*) It seems you've already got it.

Jim Did you speak?

Willie Yes. From what I heard you've had your thanks.

Jim Thanks! Is it thanks for the hospitality given to you here you're talking about? But don't think there's anything else coming to you. Despite your compliments about the nice hair and the dress. You've had all you'll get.

Tom He is our guest. I have invited him to stay.

Jim I am telling him to go. You're in a great position to be inviting guests. Guests in the house mean more money out of here. (*Indicates his pocket. To Liz*) And I'm telling you to get back to your room, put your hair back in a decent condition, take off that show-off dress. There's no Dublin Liam to admire you. This fellow (*Indicates Willie*) will be out of here in a minute and there'll be no eyes then to think you look great. You dress the way you should, miss, decent, respectable. Into your room! Now!

Willie (*Quietly*) Do not go into your room.

Jim (*Swinging round on Willie*) Did you say a word?

Willie (*Quietly*) I told her not to go to her room. She looks terrific.

Tom (*Quietly*) The look of her mother.

Jim Her mother? Terrific? What sort of indecent talk is that? (*Loud to Liz*) Into your room!

Liz (*Quietly*) No.

Jim No – what – no? (*Moving to Liz*) I'll show you no.

Tom Leave her.

Willie (*Quietly*) Do not touch her.

Jim (*To Willie*) You! No more from you! You hear?

Tom (*Upset*) Our – our guest –

Jim Guest – nothing! He's out! (*Shouting at Willie*) Get out!

Tom (*Loud*) He's not out! I have – yes – I have a job for him.

Jim Job? Job?

Tom I have asked him to do a job.

Jim I do the jobs round here.

Tom Not this job.

Jim Spouting shagging drama? That's not a job!

Tom What I have asked him to do is a very big job.

Jim What job – what?

Tom To decorate the Corner. That job.

Jim I'm decorating the Corner. I know what's to be done over there – for you, old man.

Tom No, not for me.

Jim Oh, yes, for when herself and myself –

Tom Not herself and yourself – no – no – (*Indicates Willie*) himself – staying – decorating – make it nice – and as long as he likes – stay – as long as he –

Jim As long as he – ?

Tom My house – my daughter's house – and you – she told you – out – go – you – you rated me – aye – rated me about my moneys and my – out of my house – forever gone from here – 'cause I – have I still – borne it – your insults – your low words – borne it with a patient shrug – for – for –

Willie (*Quietly*) For sufferance is the badge of all our tribe.

Tom Aye – the badge – our tribe – and your tribe – in the next field – sufferance – that's the word – sufferance – that's the word – (*He sits, exhausted. Pause. Liz gets a whiskey bottle from a cupboard, pours a little into a glass, gives it to Tom*)

Liz Here, Daddy. Take it easy. Drink this. (*Tom sips the drink*)

Jim (*Going up to Willie*) I'll do for you. Since you – it's all been – since – since then. Tinker man!

Willie (*Moving away from Jim*) Why, look you, how you storm! I would be friends with you and have your love. Forget the shames that you have stained me with. And you'll not hear me. This is kind I offer.

Tom (*Quietly*) This were kindness.

Willie And this kindness will I show. (*Turning to Tom*) I accept your offer of the job. I will decorate the Corner.

Song – "Magic Moments" (Perry Como) – comes in.

Blackout

ACT TWO

Next afternoon. Liz, hair up, working clothes on, looks "ordinary" again.

Tom He's made a great start.

Liz He has ideas about making it into three rooms over there.

Tom Well, there are three solid spaces. And good thick walls between them. Did I get him, d'you think, enough paint?

Liz Easy to get more if he needs it. He sees it all white. Three white rooms.

Tom What would I want with three white rooms when my own home is here?

Liz Your own home *is* here.

Tom Aye, for how much longer?

Liz For as long as you live.

Tom That won't be long with that fellow's hassle. And if yourself and him –

Liz If – if! Did you not hear what I said two days ago?

Tom I did. But they were words in the heat of an hour.

Liz Heat or cold, I said I was going back on everything.

Tom Aye, but will he let you?

Liz I'm not sold in slavery to him.

Tom (*Quietly*) At times I wonder about that.

Liz Well, wonder no more!

Tom There'll be trouble.

Liz Whenever isn't there with that lad? But facing up to the trouble might – you know – shake us free of him.

Tom Will we ever shake free of him?

Liz Once I thought we never would. Now –

Tom Now?

Liz Now I think there's a chance we might.

Tom What brought that chance about?

Liz (*Gesturing towards the main door UL*) D'you think himself might have had something to do with it?

Tom Liam?

Liz Not Liam! Whenever do we see Liam? Liam stepped out of our lives years ago.

Tom A pity he did.

Liz Oh, Daddy, don't walk down that old road again. I am referring to our painter across in the Corner.

Tom He's not a painter. He's an actor.

Liz Whatever he is, he might give us –

Tom What?

Liz I don't know – might give us something.

Tom Not money, that's a sure five.

Liz Right: I don't know if he's even got the fare back to Dublin.

Tom He has to get back to Dublin. I think for a big part. Dublin's where his acting is. He can't act down here.

Liz He was acting his Shakespeare with you yesterday. Although that won't line his pockets. But it keeps you here.

Tom Keeps me here?

Liz Keeps you out of Conlon's.

Tom Why d'you think I'm ever in Conlon's?

Liz 'Cause you like the taste of John Jameson.

Tom I could taste John Jameson in my own house. I frequent that establishment, so as not to be here, because –

Liz I know. Don't upset yourself. He's not here now.

Tom Where is he? I haven't seen him all day.

Liz I don't know where he is. He might have had to go into Mullingar for something.

Tom D'you think – ?

Liz What?

Tom You know the way they say holy water keeps away evil spirits?

Liz They say that.

Tom I think himself might have the effect of keeping away *that* evil spirit.

Liz (*Laughing*) You and your evil spirits! He might be an actor, but I don't think he'd have that sort of power.

Tom No. He hasn't –

Liz What?

Tom Hard to say. There's something missing. He's not – not sure of himself.

Liz Who is, for God's sake?

Tom He doesn't mention his wife.

Liz Has he a wife?

Tom He told me he'd been in love.

Liz What were you talking about love for?

Tom Ah, we were discussing things. It came up.

Liz Whatever came up, being in love doesn't mean he has to have a wife. (*Quietly*) Many's the one who's known love without wife or husband. Go and bring him over for a cup of tea. He's been hard at it for hours.

Tom You're right. We don't want him thinking we're ill using him.

Tom goes out UL. Liz gets out mugs etc. for tea, puts them on the table. She is humming to herself one of the songs heard already on the radio. After a while Liam comes to the door UL. He has a newspaper in his hand. He stands looking at Liz, who doesn't yet see him.

Liam Nice tune.

Liz (*Still not seeing him*) I'm getting you a mug of tea.

Liam I'm not here for tea.

She swings round, sees him, puts a hand to her hair, straightens her dress, realizing she is not looking her best.

Liz Liam!

Liam (*Smiling*) No one else.

Liz God!

Liam How are you?

Liz Why didn't you let us know?

Liam Let you know what?

Liz That you were calling.

Liam Can't I call on an old neighbour without letting her know?

Liz You can, you can. Sit down.

Liam I won't. I was just crossing to Johnnie Doran's. I saw your father going over the yard. I guessed you might be on your own in the house. I took that chance.

Liz You've time for Johnnie Doran. But for us it's just a chance we might be in.

Liam A chance *you* might be in. Normally when I call your father is here.

Liz It's his house.

Liam These days it seems it's someone else's house too.

Liz No, no one else's house. Just my father's and mine.

Liam Yes. (*Pause*) I promised to show Johnnie this article (*Indicates the newspaper*) about Canada.

Liz Johnnie was years in Canada.

Liam He didn't stay. Went away, came back worked the farm.

Liz (*Quietly*) Some never came back.

Liam You know why I never came back.

Liz (*Speaking in a rush*) Maybe you weren't the man to come back and fight for what you wanted.

Liam Did *you* fight for what you wanted? From what I hear, what you wanted changed rapidly after I left.

Liz Well, you left and there's an end of it.

Liam It wasn't the end of it.

Liz (*Loud: upset*) Yes, it was! It was! Things end. They can't be brought back. You left. No: you ran. Left me here. Left me adrift. And now you keep coming back. Why do you keep coming back? Why do you do that?

Liam My brother's across the field.

Liz (*Upset*) Come back for your brother, come back for Johnnie Doran, come back for my father, but –

Liam But what?

Liz (*Quietly*) But don't come back for me.

Liam It's you I always come back for, Liz.

Liz (*Quietly*) Don't! Don't come back for me.

Liam O.K. (*He walks around*) This kitchen. And that cross over the door. (*Indicates Liz's room door right*) The straw Celtic cross. An crois. It was the first time I'd ever seen one.

Liz (*Quietly*) It was my mother's.

Liam I know it was. How did I know that?

Liz You knew everything about us.

Liam I thought I did. That cross has been hanging there since your mother was a little girl. When I'd call here for you it would be the first thing I'd look at. Friday nights: the pictures in Mullingar and walks up the river, the dances in the hall. I'd bring you home and look up at the cross. An crois.

Liz (*Quietly*) It's there still. It's always there.

Liam It is. (*Pause. He walks around*) Why was that such a happy time? Why did no one say on one of those Friday nights: This is the happiest time you'll ever have in your whole life? Why did no one say that?

Liz It didn't need to be said.

Liam It didn't. Aye: I wasn't the man. You're right. I'm sorry.

Liz Sorry makes nothing happen. Sorry is only a word.

Liam I teach words. You know, poetry, with the children in school. Some of them write grand stuff. And poetry out of books. They like to pick a poem from a book and read it out loud. You'd laugh at some of the things they pick. One poem a boy chose, a well known poem. But it wasn't that poem that took my eye. It was the poem on the opposite page. I'd never come across it before. While the lad was reading, I read the poem across the page to myself. It kept going round my head.

Liz Let it stay in your head. I don't want to hear it.

Liam (*Quietly*) Their short time together
marked their best years,
loving each other
they forgot future fears.
But the future came down
like black clouds in the sky –

Liz Did you not hear me? I don't want to –

Liam – and love was the gateway
to a silent goodbye.
And when they looked back –

Liz (*Loud*) Don't look back! You can't look back!

Liam – they counted the cost,
and saw through the years

the thing they had lost.

(*Pause: quietly*) That was the poem I was looking at while the boy was speaking *his* poem. (*He looks at her*) Yeah, that was it. (*He goes out UL*)

Liz (*Very quietly*) No, never do that. Never look back.

She turns on the radio. Song: "Who's Sorry Now?" – Connie Francis. During the song she fiddles with cups, saucers, then flings a saucer on the table and sits. She listens to the song. After a while Willie appears at the door UL in old shirt and trousers, bits of white paint on the trousers. He stands looking at Liz. They stay like that for a while, then she senses he is there. She turns, sees him.

Liz You!

Willie Your father –

Liz (*Lost in her thoughts*) What?

Willie He sent me over for a cup of tea.

Liz Tea? Yes – O.K. (*She gets the kettle*) Fill this. (*He takes the kettle, goes out UL. She busies herself with teapot etc. Willie comes back with the kettle, stands UL*) What are you standing there for? Put it on the fire. It won't boil with you holding it like an amadan.

Willie (*Putting kettle on the fire*) Are you all right?

Liz (*Turning off the radio*) Who's all right? Are *you* all right? No work, your tour ended. Why do you keep asking if people are all right? No, I'm not all right. And *you're* not all right.

Willie I'm –

Liz You and your Shakespeare! What has Shakespeare to do with anyone down this way? And poetry! What *is* poetry? All that rubbish!

Willie A lot of it is rubbish – yes.

Liz Rubbish and blather! All words. Words in the head. Words in books. Words are nothing. They're not real. They're substitutes for what's real. Do you know what's real?

Willie No.

Liz What's real is something else. Work. Keeping a place going. Doing things you hate doing. Putting up with things you hate. Giving yourself up to other people. The moon shining on a boy and a girl down a country lane. That's poetry.

Willie It sounds like poetry.

Liz But life that has to be lived is not poetry. Life that has to be lived is the stink in fields in winter mud. And rain pelting down trying to scrape spuds out of the ground. And the smell of cows and pigs and blood running out of them when the knife goes in. The howl of animals in pain in a slaughter house. That's real, it's what we do here in Westmeath. None of that goes into poetry. Where's your Shakespeare when you're up to your knees in that blood and mess?

Willie Maybe poetry softens the blood and the mess.

Liz (*Loud*) It doesn't soften it! Nothing softens it. I heard my father with poetry. I listened. I thought – yes, I thought – but – no – nothing softens it. Nothing.

Willie (*Quietly*) He's been here, hasn't he? I saw him cross the yard. I guessed it was him. Does he know the effect it has on you coming back? (*She doesn't answer: pause*) I know why he comes back. I know that pull.

Liz What pull?

Willie The pull that never lets go.

Liz What would you know about that or about any pull? What have you? Have you a wife? What are you, for God's sake? Don't talk to me about all that. The pull that never lets go! Are those words from one of your plays?

Willie No.

Liz Your plays – poetry – and Shakespeare – since – since –

Willie Since what?

Liz Since you came –

Willie I've only been here two days.

Liz Two days too long! Go back to Dublin. Back to your plays and your Shakespeare.

Willie Your father asked me – the painting beyond –

Liz We'll finish the painting ourselves. You've knocked everything upside down. Thrashed things about. We were all right.

Willie Were you?

Liz We were, we were. We were set.

Willie Concrete is set.

Liz Concrete is solid. We were solid. We knew where we were. Then you came.

Willie I didn't mean to come. Yours was the first house I saw when I was dropped off. I asked how to get to Dublin.

Liz Now you know how to get to Dublin. Go back there – the whole lot of you! You're not wanted here. None of you are wanted. Whatever way you found us, leave us. Leave us the way we were. Just leave us.

Tom (*Coming in UL*) His eminence has arrived. He's got out of his car.

Liz Where has he been to?

Tom I don't know where the hell he's been to.

Jim (*Entering triumphantly*) I'll tell you where I've been to. (*During Jim's speeches, Willie is very still*) I've been all the way to Sligo. Got up early and drove the eighty miles to Sligo town. I asked around if anyone knew of a travelling theatre company in the vicinity. Still in Sligo all this week. (*Pulling a rolled poster from his pocket. Reading:*) The Monahan Players. A different play every night. The Town Hall, Sligo. Performances begin at eight p.m. sharp. Monday Jane Eyre, Tuesday The School for Scandal, Matinee Wednesday As You Like It, then the brilliant comedy The Importance of Being Earnest, Pygmalion, Macbeth, An Ideal Husband and to finish the week the magnificent drama of horror Dracula. (*Giving the poster* *to Liz*) There! Have a look at that! (*Liz looks at the poster. To Willie:*) Would you like to throw your eye over it, sir?

Tom I would like very much to throw my eye over it. (*Tom takes the poster, reads it*)

Liz (*To Willie*) You said the tour was ended.

Jim Oh, by no means has the tour ended. In fact, the Monahan Players are only halfway through their tour, which was going very well, until suddenly they had big problems on their hands when – ah – a certain actor walked out on them, without a minute's warning, leaving them with only a few hours to put on a play with one of their main actors disappeared into thin air.

Liz How do you know all this?

Jim Mr Harris told me.

Liz Who's Mr Harris?

Jim (*To Willie*) Tell them who Mr Harris is. (*Pause*) You don't want to tell them? Well, *I'll* tell them.

Tom I don't want to hear who this Mr Harris is.

Jim I think you do. Mr Harris is a soft spoken Englishman and he is the manager of the Monahan Players. A man called Matthew Monahan is the main actor – he owns the company. You see: I did my detective work well.

Tom Who the hell cares about your detective work?

Jim (*Indicates Liz*) She cares. I care. You should care, old man. You should care about the sort of fellow you allow off the street into your house.

Tom (*Upset*) I have – I have been honoured having him in my house.

Jim (*Laughing*) You'll be even more honoured hearing the end of my story.

Tom Damn the end of your story!

Jim You can damn it all you like, but this is the tale I got from Mr Harris. He told me your man here, who's taken the two of ye in, messed up the plays for the last few weeks, because he got all his lines wrong. That's what they call what they say in a play – lines.

Tom We know that, you bloody fool!

Jim If you get your lines wrong in a play, Mr Harris said, the whole thing goes down the drain. Am I not right, Mr Actor, sir? The other actors had to keep the thing going by saying his lines for him.

Liz Get on with it! Say what you have to say.

Jim What I have to say is this. They should have sacked him, Mr Harris said, but Matthew Monahan was more than generous to him and kept him on. That was a stupid thing to do, according to Mr Harris, because, next thing, in fact this week, without a nod or a goodbye he vanished into the far horizon, leaving the Monahan Players in the worst crisis they'd ever found themselves. And now comes the interesting bit.

Tom We don't want to hear your damn bit, interesting or not.

Jim (*Laughing*) Well, here it is anyway. The reason, according to Mr Harris, for all his messing up the plays, not remembering his lines – you know – was to do with the missus.

Liz Whose missus?

Jim (*Indicating Willie*) *His* missus.

Liz (*To Willie*) So you *are* married?

Jim Oh, indeed and he is! She is an actress in the company too. But now – hear this –

Tom (*Loud*) I don't want to hear this or anything else. It's the man's private business. How dare you go nosing into the man's private affairs?

Jim Private, but public as well. Because he messed up things for other people. Just as you're letting him mess up things for us here.

Tom He's messed nothing up here. Anything messed up here has not been done by him.

Jim Mr Harris said –

Tom (*Upset*) No one wants to hear what he said!

Jim The missus fell for another fellow.

Tom (*Loud*) That has nothing to do with us!

Jim This other fellow is the stage manager in the company. Oh, a fine looking lad, Mr Harris said, a great build of a young man from the County Cork. Instead of sharing digs with himself here, the missus moved into digs every week with the young stage manager. This upset our friend here so much, he couldn't remember his words in the plays. And then – this week – now what was the word Mr Harris said it was? Aye, aye, the word was scarpered. Your man here scarpered. Leaving unpaid rent for his digs and money not paid back that he'd borrowed from the company. (*Laughing*) Ah, but, sure, maybe it's understandable, it isn't the nicest thing, I would think, to see your missus going night after night to another man's bed. Especially a fine cut of a young lad from the County Cork.

Liz (*After a pause: quietly to Willie*) Is this true?

Tom (*Loud*) 'Course it's not true! This fellow's dug up a pack of lies to blacken the man's name.

Liz (*Quietly to Willie*) Is it true?

Willie (*Very quiet*) Yes.

Liz All true about messing up the plays?

Willie (*Quiet*) Yes.

Liz And about your wife?

Willie Yes.

Liz And leaving unpaid rent behind you?

Willie Yes.

Jim Of course it's true. Sure, I had it all from Mr Harris beyond in Sligo town.

Tom (*Near to tears*) God damn Sligo town!

Jim Oh, it's Sligo town now where that Monahan company are doing their best to keep afloat, despite the damage done to them and it's in Sligo town where a strapping young Cork lad shares a bed with the great actor's missus!

Liam (*Appearing at door UL*) God save the company.

Liz (*Taken by surprise*) Liam!

Tom (*Quietly pleased to see him*) Liam – Liam!

Liam Just on my way home from Johnnie Doran's. Dropped in to say au revoir to you all. Back to Dublin in the morning.

Tom But we'll be seeing you soon again, Liam?

Liam Ah – no, I don't think so, Tom.

Tom No?

Liam No. It's not just au revoir, Tom. It's more of a goodbye.

Liz Goodbye?

Liam Aye. We're heading out to Australia.

Liz What?

Liam Great opportunities there these days, they tell me. Ah, Dublin, the teaching, it's not what I – I've had the teaching: big louts squaring up to you, insolence all over their faces. (*Looking at Liz*) Here – Ireland – nothing here now. For me.

Jim Australia? That's great news! Good luck out there.

Liam I was here to tell you all this earlier, Tom, but Liz and myself got talking – aye, we got talking – and – you know the way it is – it never came out. Well, it's out now.

Jim It is, it is, so, all the best – all the best – you'll want to be getting back to your brother's now.

Liam I wanted you to know in this house – Tom – Liz.

Tom Ah, it's not goodbye, surely, is it, Liam?

Liam I'm afraid so, Tom. Australia is a far away country.

Jim Yes, yes, we wish you all the best, thanks for calling –

Tom One thing, Liam.

Liam Aye, Tom?

Tom Don't – don't say goodbye. I hate goodbyes.

Liam I won't say goodbye, Tom. I'll just say – (*He sees Willie*) Good Christ, is that who I think it is? (*He takes a step to Willie*)

Tom (*Pleased Liam has recognized Willie*) That's who it is, Liam.

Liam In workman's gear. Is it for a part you're dressed like that?

Jim This lad is always dressed for a part. The part that dodges the truth and pulls the wool over people's eyes.

Liam (*Staring at Willie*) William Walsh! By Jesus, I've seen you in some great plays in Dublin.

Tom (*Pleased*) I bet you have, Liam!

Liam This guy was a bloody top man in Dublin when I was training and after I started teaching up there. I saw him in hundreds of plays. (*To Willie*) Your wife was with you in a lot of the plays. Ann Scott: that's his wife, Tom.

Tom Yes?

Jim Oh, yes, the wife, the wife!

Liam Christ, they were superb together. Fitted each other like a glove on the stage. And – and that play – that new play I saw you

164

in that – about the fellow that was a great hurler and couldn't face it that he was past it. You should have seen that play, Tom, your man here was terrific in it.

Tom I would expect nothing less.

Liam And what are you doing in this neck of the woods?

Jim This neck of the woods has had more than enough of him. He was touring with a company in Sligo and he –

Liam Touring in Sligo? So that's what you've been doing – touring. Aye, I hadn't noticed you in anything in Dublin these last few years. Funny enough, we were talking about you the other night – myself and Jackie Regan. Jackie trained with me. We often sat in the gods in the Gaiety together. Christ, Jackie thought you were the best ever.

Tom I bet he did!

Liam Anything you were in Jackie was off to see you. And when you were with Ann Scott –

Jim Oh, he was with her all right. And he was with her in Sligo. (*To Willie*) Were you not?

Liam But, God Almighty, what were you doing in Sligo? You belong in Dublin. The Dublin theatre: that's your place. Synge, Shakespeare, O'Casey, new plays. And that play about the hurler – you and your wife together –

Jim Oh, ho, the wife and himself together!

Liam The two of them together – aye.

Jim Together! Yes, oh, yes!

Liam By God, didn't they make the sparks fly!

Jim (*Laughing*) Made the sparks fly, did they – what?

Liam By Christ, they did!

Jim Sparks! Oh, aye, sparks! Him and the wife together – sparks!

Willie (*Suddenly erupting*) Sparks! What, Jim? What? You too made sparks. You have done well. You have dug – delved – turned up all – you have, good man! – discovered – detected – explored – unearthed – excavated and located –

Jim I located all about you, me brave bucko!

Willie Go to, then –

Jim I will not go to! Don't friggin' tell me to go to!

Willie You come to me and you say – you have brought the good news – crept in – crept out – as is your wont – oh, yes, middle of the night – creep in – creep out – many a time and oft –

Liam That's Willie Walsh all right!

Willie Go to, then –

Jim (*Shouting*) I'll break your fucking neck if you tell me to go to again!

Willie Shall I bend low – and in a bondman's key say this – yes – walked out – unpaid rent – money subbed not repaid – all that – yes – left all in the – left all behind – gone now – all gone now – so with bated breath – and whispering humbleness – (*To Liz*) what should I say to you?

Jim You say fuck all!

Willie (*To Liz*) I say this: your bed is yours – you say no to your bed –

Jim What's any of that to you, you bloody – ?

Willie Well, then –

Tom Well, then – what?

Liz Yes – what?

Tom (*Almost breaking down*) What are we to do? What?

Willie You come to me and you say – what to do?

Tom What? What?

Willie What is obvious.

Tom Obvious?

Willie Sell.

Liz Sell?

Willie House – land –

Tom Land – house – ?

Willie Move.

Tom Move where?

Willie (*Pointing*) There!

Liam The Corner!

Jim (*Indicates Tom*) That's where he's going.

Tom That's where they're shoving me.

Willie No! No shoving. Living! (*To Tom*) The Corner for you – (*To Liz*) and for you – oh, yes, indeed – you come to me and you say – what to do? – I say this – up goes the For Sale sign – but –

Liz But?

Willie – a most important but –

Tom What – but?

Willie (*Indicates Jim*) It must not go to him – you know the law –

Tom The law? What do you mean?

Liam He means what he's telling you.

Liz (*To Liam*) What is he telling us? What?

Liam Sell up. The land, the house, move to the Corner. But with the strict condition.

Liz Condition?

Willie (*Putting up a finger*) Strict.

Liam Condition. (*Indicates Jim*) None of it can be bought by him.

Jim I'm in here – by Jaysus, I am!

Liam And you'll be out of here.

Jim No one'll put me out! I've got my place here now.

Willie The law does not say so.

Jim Frig the law! The money I put in –

Liam They'll pay you back your money. (*To Tom*) That's what he's saying. (*Indicates Willie*)

Jim Who's he to bloody say anything?

Liam He's Willie Walsh, Dublin actor. That's who he is. And that's what he's saying. With a bit of help from Shakespeare.

Jim Shag Shakespeare!

Willie Yes, yes, more than a few Elizabethan ladies had that pleasure.

Jim No one'll put me out this door!

Liam You're half out already. I was here when you came in. I thank God I'm here to see you put out.

Jim (*Shouting*) I'll not be put out! I'll get my right!

Willie (*To Tom*) Indeed, you know the law. Your exposition hath been most sound.

Tom Very sound. Yes, by God – out – he'll be out. (*To Willie*) You'll do it – good man – you will –

Tom takes Willie by the arm, they circle Jim, as in a dance. They get into a dance rhythm.

– holy water – drive him out – holy water – out – out – power of the water – drive him out –

Jim (*Confused, retreating to the door UL, still being circled by Tom and Willie*) What – the name of Jaysus – ?

Tom (*Circling Jim with Willie*) Out – out – drive him out – holy water – drive him out –

Jim (*showing some fear at the mention of holy water*) Holy water? That – that kind of talk – it's not right –

Tom (*Circling Jim, moving towards the door UL*) Holy water – holy water – drive him out – holy water – drive him out –

Jim No – in a Christian house – that sort of sinful talk –

Tom (*Circling Jim: they are now at the door*) Power of the water – out – out –

Jim (*Loud: unnerved*) Unchristian – that's what it is –

Tom – holy water – drive him out –

Jim – out – aye – but I'll be back – by Christ I'll be back –

Jim turns and stumbles out the door. Tom and Willie stand still. They are breathing heavily. Silence. Everyone is still. Long pause. Then:

Liam (*Very quietly*) No, I won't say goodbye. You're right, Tom, goodbyes are – too many goodbyes. (*He walks to Liz's bedroom door R, looks at the Celtic cross over the door*) I'll always remember this house. And the straw Celtic cross over the door. An crois. All the nights – all the – that happy time. (*Slight pause*)

Tom Come on, Liam, I'll walk with you to Paddy's. Many's the time and oft I walked that same field with you when you were a gossoon. As you said, Australia is a step far away. So, most likely, you won't be greeting your old neighbour when you come again.

Liam Oh, now, Tom –

Tom No blame to anyone, Liam. Life has its own ways. So we'll take our walk. A walk across a field. What better way to wave a man off on his journey to Australia?

Liam (*Looking at Liz, who is very still. She is not looking at Liam*) Yeah. Come on, then. We'll do that. We'll take our walk across the field.

Tom and Liam go out. Long pause. Liz and Willie are standing, not looking at each other.

Liz (*Speaks quietly*) Walked out? (*No reply from him*) Left everyone in a mess? (*No reply*) Left debts behind you? (*No reply. she speaks louder*) And – and all that talk – big talk – plays in Dublin – great jobs – it was all – all – (*A cynical little laugh*) and the joke's on us – for we thought we were looking up at something.

Willie It was yourselves were desperate to look up at something.

Liz Right. We were aching to see something beyond ourselves. And what did we see? A defrauder of decent people. A cardsharp and a rogue. Nothing there but big talk and oul' raimeis. Seafoid agus raimeis! (*Very upset*) Sin anois! (*Loud*) Get out! Out! Out of the house! (*She is crying quietly*)

Willie I will. (*Slight pause*) And you might as well know it wasn't a friend dropped me off on the road. I hitch hiked. Picked up a lift this side of Sligo. (*Pause*) So there, you have it all now. (*Pause. He does not move*)

Liz I have too much! (*Pause: turns to him*) What are you waiting for?

Willie I suppose – waiting to say goodbye.

Liz We hate goodbyes down here. You heard my father.

Willie I won't say goodbye, then.

Liz Don't. Just go.

Willie I will. (*Moving*) So long.

Liz And you can keep your so longs as well – that's the same language as goodbye. So long, goodbye! They're your words for everyone. Walking away, never staying at anything. Taking, but never giving. Pretending – letting on you could do something – give people something.

Willie I can't.

Liz You tricked us into thinking you could. You let my father think you could. Kept him here in the house instead of drink rotting down in the pub. All that Shakespeare nonsense with him –

Willie Nonsense? Aye, maybe you're right.

Liz (*Slumping on to a chair*) Ah, when the hell was I ever right about anything? Was I right when I let that spade handle of a neighbour into my bed – when I let him break into the one happy time I had in my life?

Willie If I could do something for you and Tom, I would. But I haven't got – whatever it is. You mustn't think I've got that. I haven't.

Liz No, you haven't. Nor would you even try for such a thing.

Willie Try?

Liz Yes! My father. That old man. Giving him something, then taking it from him again.

Willie I wouldn't.

Liz Yes, you would! You'd walk out on him too. Like you walk out on everyone. Leave us on our own – to be pushed down in the mud again by – by –

Willie By?

Liz You know! (*Quietly*) My father said you were the holy water keeping him out.

Willie There's no holy water in me, Liz.

Liz If there isn't, then it's the end of us.

Willie Of course it isn't. You never listened, did you?

Liz I listened to you for too long an hour.

Willie You listened, but you didn't hear.

Liz I heard! And all I heard was rubbish.

Willie Well, here's more of that rubbish: sell.

Liz Sell?

Willie The house, the land. Make it a condition he can't be the buyer. Pay him back what he's owed from the price you get. Keep the Corner. Move into it. There's room over there for a nice dwelling.

Liz We saw it only as a put out for my father.

Willie More than that. Three good rooms.

Liz Three good rooms and a kitchen space.

Willie There you have it. Something came out of the rubbish after all.

Liz We couldn't see what was staring us in the face. A nice dwelling with three rooms.

Willie A lovely dwelling. If the work is put in on it.

Liz (*Quietly*) Yes! (*Slowly*) A lovely dwelling.

Willie Lovely. (*Moves to door*) I'll collect my bag beyond.

Liz Collect your bag? (*Pause. Quieter*) Oh, indeed! And leave us to live like cows in a cattle shed in that dwelling.

Willie Why d'you have to live like cows in a cattle shed?

Liz We'll be cows in a cattle shed and the job over there making it into a nice dwelling not finished.

Willie Get it finished.

Liz Who got it started?

Willie (*Slight pause*) You told me to get out.

Liz Oh, yes, get out! Run! That's your rule in life. Can't you ever finish a thing for once in your life?

Willie I've finished whatever there was here.

Liz There's not much here. There'll be even less if the Corner isn't painted out. But much you'll care about the painting or about us when you're back in Dublin.

Willie What's in Dublin?

Liz Lots in Dublin. Buses and cars, taxis, exhaust fumes. Shops and rushing people. Jackeen gurriers running round the place. And the smell of the Liffey.

Willie I miss that smell.

Liz You miss the smell of your acting too. I don't know what sort of performer you are on the stage. But you're a bad one off it, trying to hide that obvious thing.

Willie Obvious?

Liz Very obvious. Liam said –

Willie Forget what Liam said.

Liz In Dublin he saw you in plays.

Willie (*Loudly, swinging round on her*) Plays! The long road to Dublin is longer than you think. I could not step out on a stage now. You people don't know what I'm taking about. You're farming people. This is when your head goes empty in front of three or four hundred punters under stage lights and actors round you wondering what the hell's happened to you. Your mind empty and your tongue like a hard rock that won't move, not getting a word out. And you go down to the lowest rung of humiliation. That's what happened to me in Sligo. It happened to me in Bundoran the week before. And in Ballyshannon. It's why I was here painting your outhouse for a night's sleep. It's why you were able to call me a cardsharp and a rogue. It's why Jim can treat me like the tinker off the roads he said I was. Being in a play again? No! It's gone.

Liz What goes can come back.

Willie I don't want it back!

Liz Don't you? Yeah, we are farming people. Maybe I don't know what you're talking about. But I saw my father – this – (*She gets the Shakespeare book from the shelf, taps it*)

Willie That? Five minutes happy with Shakespeare! What is that, for Christ sake? Did Shakespeare banish the lack of harmony in this house? Did it keep your neighbour out of your bed? Did it stop you and Liam breaking apart? Will it stop Tom losing his home if you and Jim –

Liz (*Slapping the book on the table*) Me and Jim! That is not to happen.

Willie Happen or not, you said it yourself: all that is not real. Real is elsewhere. Real is Jim coming to you in the middle of the night. It's Tom wasting his days down in the pub. It's me in Sligo, the clown of the company, because my wife is tumbling with a fellow half my age in their digs.

Liz And what Liam saw in Dublin – your acting – was not that real?

Willie (*More calm*) Once I thought it was the only thing that *was* real. Hours in pubs and cafes and talk about theatre (pronounced "the-ah-tah") and truth onstage and motivation and the inner life of the characters and the subtext and this text and that text. Utter crap! Great productions, marvellous performances, we thought were essential to the working of the world. But great performances didn't stop people crying out in pain in hospital beds.

Liz Digging spuds in muddy fields doesn't stop people crying out in pain in hospital beds either.

Willie Digging spuds in fields feeds people.

Liz A bit of enjoyment from a play might feed them too.

Willie Doubtful. I saw good actors, magnetic on stage, cheered to the roof by a packed house. When it was all over and we'd gone home, what difference did it make? Most of the audience didn't remember what they were cheering two weeks later. Oh, great, I get back my confidence and give a performance again in Dublin that some Guinness filled hack, demoted from covering the dog races at Harold's Cross, says was "really quite good". After his paper is wrapped round a pound of chops by a Mullingar butcher, what will it mean? Nothing. Not a bloody thing.

Liz (*Quietly after a pause*) Well, goodbye then. Goodbye to your acting. And goodbye to us down here. We thought for a while there was – I don't know – yes, we let ourselves think that. But there was nothing. You'd best be off then before my father comes back.

Willie He'll be all right.

Liz Will he?

Willie He will. And you'll be all right yourself.

Liz I have your assurance for that, have I? Did you tell the actors in Sligo they'd be all right before you walked out on them and left them in a mess?

Willie (*Quietly*) No.

Liz No. Then don't tell me I'll be all right. Who the hell's all right in this life? And those actors you walked out on, traipsing round the country, in digs, away from their families. I know feck all about acting or your theatres – ask me about onions and I'll talk all day about onions – but don't tell me those actors in Sligo think what they do amounts to nothing. I don't know what it amounts to, but it must be there for something. God Almighty, I still remember the great laughs I had at the St Patrick Players with Paddy Breen acting the eejit falling off tables and that was ten or more years ago. Something stays, something sticks.

Willie (*A slight pause: quietly*) I can't do it any more, Liz.

Liz Maybe you can't, but others can. And they might light up some dark corner deep inside us. A murky space that needs a bit of a shine thrown on it. Getting lost in laughs or tied up in a story for an hour is often what keeps us going down here. (*Indicating the Shakespeare book on the table*) I suppose there's a few laughs and stories even in this. My father seems able to weed them out. But they're buried too far down in all those twisted words for me to be able to make anything out of them. Mind you, it wasn't for laughs or stories I put it under the leg of my dressing table to steady it for six months. (*Pointing*) There's the mark still!

Jim appears at the door UL with the Sergeant.

Jim (*Pointing*) There's your man, Sergeant.

Sergeant Thank you. I'm sorry, Elizabeth, for this intrusion.

Liz Intrusion? Why?

Jim Why d'you think?

Sergeant I am instructed to follow up an allegation.

Jim (*Pointing at Willie*) Against him! Against that fella!

Sergeant (*Coming down to Willie*) William Walsh?

Willie (*Quietly*) Yes.

Sergeant I'd like to talk to you, Mr Walsh, about money that was left owing in Sligo.

Liz (*To Jim as she gets up*) You did this.

Jim The people have to get their money restored to them, haven't they? Everyone must get what's theirs!

Sergeant Complaints have been made against you, Mr Walsh.

Jim Two complaints!

Sergeant Two complaints. (*Looking at a piece of paper*) A Mrs Redmond in Sligo claims she agreed to give you lodgings for a week at four pounds rent.

Jim Four pounds rent she never saw.

Sergeant Even though only part of the week was completed, the agreement was for a full week. Therefore, Mrs Redmond is entitled to four pounds. And I understand you subbed money out of your wages from the company that employed you.

Jim The Monahan Players employed him. He owes them six pounds ten shillings. I got it all from Mr Harris.

Sergeant That is correct. The company claims six pounds and ten shillings.

Jim Four pounds for the lodgings and six pounds ten for Mr Harris. The total being ten pounds and ten shillings. (*Laughing*) I was always good at my sums!

Sergeant Now, if you'll come with me, Mr Walsh, I'll take a statement from you down in the barracks.

Liz There will be no need for the barracks, Sergeant.

Sergeant No?

Liz Nor for any statement.

Jim There *is* need for a statement, there is, there is. A statement about the money he left owing.

Liz That money will be paid.

Jim Will it, now? And who'll pay it – ha? Who?

Liz I will.

Sergeant *You* will, Elizabeth?

Liz Yes. (*She goes into her room R*)

Jim (*Calling after her*) You will? You're not going to waste that money on – that's yours for –

Liz (*From the room*) That's mine for paying what I want to pay.

Jim (*Calling to Liz*) What you want to pay? (*To Sergeant*) I have claims on that money, Sergeant.

Sergeant You have, Jim?

Jim I shaggin' well have! Any money in this house came from – from what I put in here. I have a say over that money.

Liz (*Coming in counting pound notes*) One – two – three – (*Then quietly until*) – ten pounds –

Jim You're not flinging away good money for that – tramp – (*Gestures towards Willie*) – that –

Liz And ten shillings. (*Holding out the notes*) There's your money, Sergeant.

Sergeant Are you quite sure about this, Elizabeth?

Liz I am, Sergeant.

Jim She's not, no, she's not! She's squandering money you could say belongs to me.

Sergeant Belongs to you, Jim?

Jim She wouldn't have a penny if I hadn't worked day and night pulling this farm out of the mud.

Sergeant That may be so. But let us be clear about this: whose money is this I'm holding in my hand?

Liz It's my money, Sergeant.

Sergeant If you say so, Elizabeth, that's good enough for me.

Jim It's not good enough for me! That fella has to go to the barracks for defrauding people out of what they're owed.

Sergeant But the money has been repaid, Jim. I have it here in my hand. (*Holding up the money*) Of course if the people in Sligo who were owed the money wish to press charges, then it's out of my hands.

Jim I'll get on to them in Sligo. I'll see they press charges.

Sergeant That's up to you. (*Turns to Liz*) I've known you, Elizabeth, since you were a girl. I've known Tom, your father. This has always been a decent house, with decent people in it. The last thing I'd wish would be to bring trouble into this house.

Jim (*Pointing to Willie*) It's him that's brought trouble into this house. Him! That feckin' trickster!

Sergeant No, I don't wish to bring trouble here. Because of that, because the lady of this house wishes for the money to be repaid, I will recommend that no further action is taken against Mr Walsh. (*He moves, then turns back*) And, by the way, Mr Walsh, I once saw you in The Playboy of the Western World in my home town of Limerick when I was back there on holiday.

Jim You saw him in Limerick! But you're not seeing what it is your duty to see. You'll take no further action! And all my journey to Sligo, all my deep enquiries to dig up the truth about this thief, to urge people to press for their money, to see justice done, is for damn all, is it?

Sergeant That's not for me to say. But isn't it great to see there are still people in this country who have such a high regard for justice. Maybe, Jim, you should be doing my job.

Jim I'd do it a bloody sight better than you, you incompetent fecker.

Sergeant Maybe so. Anyway, thank you for your help in getting the money back to where it belongs. And thank you, Elizabeth.

Liz That's all right, Sergeant.

Sergeant Again, I am sorry for the intrusion. I hope next time I call, it will be on more pleasant business. God bless you all. (*He goes*)

Jim God bless us all! Turning his back on the law and his duty, the lazy oul' bastard. (*To Liz*) And you throwing away that hard earned money on this tramp – this drifter – in off the road – a decent house – upsetting all – everything – letting this bum – this swindler of people – bring his bad ways into a Christian house – (*Snatching the Shakespeare book*) – and this – all this – (*Suddenly tearing up the book, his voice loud*) – robbing people – stealing money – turning a decent home into – into a – (*Shouting*) – thief! – robber! – defrauder of honest people! – (*He rushes to the shelf, pulls books down, starts tearing them apart*) – and this – all this – get rid of it – rid of all that – rid! – rid! – no more of this – (*Very loud, building to a climax*) no more of it – I'll hear no more – no more! – I won't – no more! –

He goes silent, breathing hard. He stands still, lets bits of books fall to the floor. He stands, arms down by his side, as if he has lost all strength. The torn books are scattered around him. A pause. Then Willie goes around Jim picking up the torn bits of books while speaking the speech very confidently and without any hesitation.

Willie Signior Antonio, many a time and oft
In the Rialto you have rated me
About my moneys and my usances.
Still have I borne it with a patient shrug,
For sufferance is the badge of all our tribe.
You call me misbeliever, cut throat dog,
And spit upon my Jewish gaberdine
And all for that which is mine own.
Well then, it now appears you need my help.
You, that did void your rheum upon my beard
And foot me as you spurn a stranger cur
Over your threshold.
I would be friends with you and have your love,
Forget the shames that you have stain'd me with.
This is kind I offer.

Pause. Willie stands very still, his hands full of the torn books. There are still bits of torn paper on the floor.

Liz (*Looking out front, very quiet, as if praying*) Holy water keep him out. Holy water, keep him out.

A torn page falls from Jim's hand. He looks around as if in a daze.

Jim Wha – ?
Liz (*Quietly to herself*) Keep him out, holy water keep him out.
Jim (*In a daze*) Out – ?

174

Liz (*Quietly to herself*) Power of the water keep him out.

Jim (*Pause. he mumbles*) Aye – my father used to say – always used to say – (*He walks slowly to the door UL*) and he was right – he was right – (*He goes out slowly. there is a pause*)

Liz Well, there! That's ten pounds ten you owe me.

Willie Yeah.

Liz It's the first time I ever paid out wages and the job still not done.

Willie I suppose I – I best get it done.

Liz Oh, I'll see you get it done, don't worry about that, me boy! We're cabbage green down here, but not as cabbage green as you think. And kidding me about the acting – not being able to do it anymore. Sure, it's all there still in your head. You just showed us how it's done. And you can do it back in Dublin too. But not before you've earned the wages I've paid you and done out the Corner for us. (*Pause. She looks at the torn paper on the floor*) And will you look at poor Shakespeare! Scattered in bits and pieces all over the place.

The song – "Catch a Falling Star" (Perry Como) – comes gently in.

Willie (*Looking at the bits of torn book in his hands*) It was a lovely book to handle.

Liz It was a lovely book to keep my dressing table steady before I got the leg mended.

Willie Well, didn't you know: scholars have proved that's why Shakespeare wrote his plays – to steady the Irish dressing tables.

Liz Sure, why else would he write them?

Song fully up.

Blackout